Literature & Thoug
GOVERNMENT AND CURRENT

INDIVIDUAL RIGHTS
THE BLESSINGS OF LIBERTY

Perfection Learning

EDITORIAL DIRECTOR	Carol Francis
EXECUTIVE EDITOR	Jim Strickler
EDITORIAL TEAM	Andrea Stark, Sheri Cooper
PERMISSIONS	Melissa Hoelker
REVIEWERS	Debra Bortzfield, Debra Robinson
ART DIRECTOR	Randy Messer
DESIGNER	Tobi Cunningham
IMAGE RESEARCH	Anjanette Houghtaling
COVER ART	© Diana Ong / Purestock / SuperStock

© 2013 Perfection Learning®
www.perfectionlearning.com
All rights reserved. No part of this book may be reproduced, stored in a retrieval system, or transmitted in any form or by any means, electronic, mechanical, photocopying, recording, or otherwise, without the prior permission of the publisher. For information regarding permissions, write to: Permissions Department, Perfection Learning, 2680 Berkshire Parkway, Des Moines, Iowa 50325.

1 2 3 4 5 6 PP 17 16 15 14 13 12

PP/Logan, Iowa, USA
3/12

94327

PB ISBN-10: 0-7891-8292-0
PB ISBN-13: 978-0-7891-8292-0
RLB ISBN-10: 1-61383-182-X
RLB ISBN-13: 978-1-61383-182-3

Printed in the United States of America

WHAT PREVENTS TYRANNY?

The question above is the essential question that you will consider as you read this book. The selections, activities, and organization of the book will lead you to think critically about this question and to develop a deeper understanding of how effectively the Constitution, Bill of Rights, and other amendments guard individual liberties.

CLUSTER ONE How would society be different without the First Amendment?
  CRITICAL THINKING SKILL EVALUATING ARGUMENTS

CLUSTER TWO How well does federalism protect individual rights?
  CRITICAL THINKING SKILL DEFINING KEY WORDS AND PHRASES

CLUSTER THREE Why are suspects' rights important?
  CRITICAL THINKING SKILL INTEGRATING MULTIMEDIA INFORMATION

CLUSTER FOUR Thinking on Your Own
  CRITICAL THINKING SKILL INTEGRATING SOURCES OF INFORMATION

Notice that the final cluster asks you to think independently about your answer to the essential question—What prevents tyranny?

We the People of the United States, in Order to form a more perfect Union, establish Justice, insure domestic Tranquility, provide for the common defense, promote the general Welfare, and **secure the Blessings of Liberty** to ourselves and our Posterity, do ordain and establish this Constitution for the United States of America.

—*Preamble to the Constitution of the United States, 1787*

The Conventions of a number of the States, having at the time of their adopting the Constitution, expressed a desire, **in order to prevent misconstruction or abuse of its powers,** that further declaratory and restrictive clauses should be added: And as extending the ground of public confidence in the Government, will best ensure the beneficent ends of its institution.

—*Preamble to the Bill of Rights, 1791*

TABLE OF CONTENTS

CLUSTER FOUR   THINKING ON YOUR OWN

THE BILL OF RIGHTS

When the Constitution was signed in September of 1787, not all the states immediately ratified it, in part because many leaders felt that it did not do enough to protect the basic rights of American citizens. In September 1789, the First Congress of the United States set about drafting a set of amendments that would spell out and secure the "certain unalienable rights" lauded in the Declaration of Independence. Congress proposed 12 amendments to the Constitution. The first two, which concerned the number of constituents for each Representative and the compensation of Congressmen, were rejected, but the other ten were ratified and eventually came to be known as the Bill of Rights.

Amendment I

Congress shall make no law respecting an establishment of religion, or prohibiting the free exercise thereof; or abridging the freedom of speech, or of the press; or the right of the people peaceably to assemble, and to petition the Government for a redress of grievances.

Amendment II

A well regulated Militia, being necessary to the security of a free State, the right of the people to keep and bear Arms, shall not be infringed.

Amendment III

No Soldier shall, in time of peace be quartered in any house, without the consent of the Owner, nor in time of war, but in a manner to be prescribed by law.

The constitutions of Mexico, Guatemala, and Haiti also protect the right to bear arms.

Amendment I

This amendment protects five fundamental freedoms: religion, speech, press, assembly, and petition. In discussions about religion and the Constitution, people often use the phrase "separation between church and state." However, this phrase is not found in the First Amendment. Thomas Jefferson coined the phrase in an 1802 letter to a group concerned about religious freedom. *(Read Jefferson's letter on page 20.)*

Unlike the United States, the People's Republic of China censors free speech and represses Internet sites it deems critical of the Chinese government.

Amendment II

Having had their guns confiscated by the British, the leaders of the new country were eager to protect their right to bear arms. Today, however, this right is a point of debate between gun control advocates and gun rights supporters. *(Read "Putting the Second Amendment Second" on page 75.)*

Amendment III

Americans resented that the King had passed laws that permitted "quartering large bodies of armed troops" in the houses of private citizens. This amendment was a direct response to this abuse.

Amendment IV

The right of the people to be secure in their persons, houses, papers, and effects, against unreasonable searches and seizures, shall not be violated, and no Warrants shall issue, but upon probable cause, supported by Oath or affirmation, and particularly describing the place to be searched, and the persons or things to be seized.

Amendment V

No person shall be held to answer for a capital, or otherwise infamous crime, unless on a presentment or indictment of a Grand Jury, except in cases arising in the land or naval forces, or in the Militia, when in actual service in time of War or public danger; nor shall any person be subject for the same offence to be twice put in jeopardy of life or limb; nor shall be compelled in any criminal case to be a witness against himself, nor be deprived of life, liberty, or property, without due process of law; nor shall private property be taken for public use, without just compensation.

Amendment VI

In all criminal prosecutions, the accused shall enjoy the right to a speedy and public trial, by an impartial jury of the State and district wherein the crime shall have been committed, which district shall have been previously ascertained by law, and to be informed of the nature and cause of the accusation; to be confronted with the witnesses against him; to have compulsory process for obtaining witnesses in his favor, and to have the Assistance of Counsel for his defence.

Amendment VII

In Suits at common law, where the value in controversy shall exceed twenty dollars, the right of trial by jury shall be preserved, and no fact tried by a jury, shall be otherwise re-examined in any Court of the United States, than according to the rules of the common law.

Amendments IV–VI

These amendments protect the rights of people suspected or accused of crimes. *(Read about the rights of suspects in Cluster Three, pages 81–109.)*

Because of the Fourth Amendment, police officers must have a reasonable belief that someone has committed a crime (probable cause), and then they usually must obtain a search warrant to search private property.

Because of the Fifth Amendment, people cannot be accused of a serious crime unless a grand jury believes there is enough evidence to warrant a trial. People cannot be charged for the same crime twice; they can't be forced to testify against themselves; and their lives, freedom, and money and belongings cannot be taken from them unless the full process of law is followed.

The Sixth Amendment outlines the rights of a person accused of a crime, including the right to a speedy and public trial by an impartial jury.

Amendment VII

Guaranteed by this amendment is the right to have a jury hear civil cases, or noncriminal lawsuits.

Amendment VIII

Excessive bail shall not be required, nor excessive fines imposed, nor cruel and unusual punishments inflicted.

Amendment IX

The enumeration in the Constitution, of certain rights, shall not be construed to deny or disparage others retained by the people.

Amendment X

The powers not delegated to the United States by the Constitution, nor prohibited by it to the States, are reserved to the States respectively, or to the people.

Protesters from the "Tea Party," a loosely-organized group of citizens opposed to big government, let the federal government know they want states' rights respected.

Amendment XIV

Section 1 All persons born or naturalized in the United States, and subject to the jurisdiction thereof, are citizens of the United States and of the State wherein they reside. No State shall make or enforce any law which shall abridge the privileges or immunities of citizens of the United States; nor shall any State deprive any person of life, liberty, or property, without due process of law; nor deny to any person within its jurisdiction the equal protection of the laws.

Section 5 The Congress shall have the power to enforce, by appropriate legislation, the provisions of this article.

Amendment VIII

In recent years, this amendment has been used to question the constitutionality of the death penalty and interrogation methods used with suspected terrorists. *(Read about the application of the Eighth Amendment to juvenile justice on pages 129–139.)*

Amendment IX

This amendment was a response to critics of the Bill of Rights. They believed that because it was impossible to list all of the rights, it would be dangerous to list some, because the government might take the opportunity to step in and abuse rights not clearly enumerated. *(Read about the first Supreme Court decision to use the Ninth Amendment as the core of its opinion on page 62.)*

Amendment X

The Tenth Amendment clarifies that the federal government retains only those powers granted by the Constitution and that all other powers not stated are given to the states or to the people.

Amendment XIV

Sections 1 and 5 of the Fourteenth Amendment are especially important in assuring that the states, not just the federal government, protect individual rights.

(Read "The Doll Test and the Fourteenth Amendment" on page 52, "Privacy and the Ninth Amendment" on page 62, and "The Civil Rights of American Muslims After 9/11" on page 91, for more on the Fourteenth Amendment and its role in protecting individual rights.)

INCORPORATION OF THE BILL OF RIGHTS TIME LINE

The Incorporation Doctrine is the process by which the Supreme Court has applied the Bill of Rights to the states. When it was ratified, the Bill of Rights applied only to the federal government. State law was regulated by each individual state's bill of rights in its own constitution. Over time, the Supreme Court began to overrule state laws that restricted the fundamental rights outlined by the Bill of Rights. The power to apply these rights flows from the due process clause found in the Fourteenth Amendment.

1873
The Slaughterhouse Cases

A local butcher in the 1880s.

Case: Claiming that their right to practice their trade was violated, twenty-five butchers filed suit when the state gave 17 people the exclusive right to operate the only slaughterhouse in New Orleans.

Ruling: The Supreme Court ruled in favor of the state, but two dissenting justices argued that the Fourteenth Amendment protects the fundamental liberties of all citizens against state interference.

Impact: This was the first time Supreme Court justices argued that the Bill of Rights should apply to the states.

1925
Gitlow v. New York

Case: Gitlow, a socialist, was convicted under a New York statute prohibiting anyone from promoting violent revolution.

Ruling: Although the Supreme Court decided that the New York law did not violate Gitlow's First Amendment right to free speech, in its opinion the Court clearly stated that freedom of speech and freedom of the press are fundamental rights protected "from impairment by the states."

Impact: Incorporated the right to freedom of speech (First Amendment)

A Chicago railroad station in 1898.

1897
Chicago B & Q v. Chicago

Case: A railroad company sued the city of Chicago when the city built a public road on the railroad's land without any remuneration.

Ruling: The Court unanimously held that the Fourteenth Amendment's due process clause requires the states to provide fair compensation when taking private property for public use.

Impact: This was the first time the Court applied the Bill of Rights to the states.

1931
Near v. Minnesota

Case: Publishers of a newspaper were convicted under a Minnesota law that targeted "malicious" and "scandalous" publications.

Ruling: The Supreme Court ruled that the Minnesota law violated the First Amendment of the Constitution.

Impact: Incorporated the right to freedom of the press (First Amendment)

You are malicious, scandalous and defamatory!

MINNESOTA

Yet protected from you by the First Amendment!

stus.com

Amendments Not Incorporated

The Third Amendment—right to freedom from housing soldiers

The Fifth Amendment—right to grand jury clause

The Seventh Amendment—right to jury trial in civil cases

The Eighth Amendment—ban on excessive fines

The Ninth Amendment—rights not specifically outlined in the Constitution

Bill of Rights

Congress of the United States,

1937
Palko v. Connecticut

Case: Frank Palko was found guilty of second-degree murder. After an appeal, he was found guilty of first-degree murder. Palko claimed he was denied his protection from double jeopardy under the Fifth Amendment.

Ruling: The Supreme Court ruled that the due process clause protects only those rights that are essential to liberty and held that the right of double jeopardy was not an essential right.

Impact: This allowed the Court to apply the Bill of Rights on a case-by-case basis, which is also called *selective incorporation*. The Court eventually overruled their original decision and incorporated protection against double jeopardy in 1969.

1948
Cole v. Arkansas

Impact: Incorporated the right to public trial (Sixth Amendment)

1948
Wolf v. Colorado

Impact: Incorporated the no unreasonable searches and seizures clause (Fourth Amendment)

1964
Malloy v. Hogan

Impact: Incorporated the no self-incrimination clause (Fifth Amendment)

1940
Cantwell v. Connecticut

Impact: Incorporated the right to free exercise of religion (First Amendment)

In the *Cantwell v. Connecticut* ruling, Justice Owen Roberts stated that a Connecticut statute requiring door-to-door religious solicitors to have a permit placed "a forbidden burden upon the exercise of liberty protected by the Constitution."

1962
Robinson v. California

Case: Under a California law making it illegal to be a drug addict, Lawrence Robinson was given a 90-day prison sentence.

Ruling: The Court held that California law violated the Constitution by punishing people for having an illness, instead of punishing them for committing a specific illegal act.

Impact: Incorporated the no cruel and unusual punishment clause (Eighth Amendment)

2010
McDonald v. Chicago

Case: A gun owner filed suit against the city of Chicago because of an ordinance that banned the possession of handguns and other weapons.

Ruling: The Court ruled that Chicago's gun regulation, in as far as it prohibited the private possession of handguns for self-defense, was a violation of the Second Amendment under the due process clause of the Fourteenth Amendment.

Impact: Incorporated the right to bear arms (Second Amendment)

Plaintiff Otis McDonald speaks outside the Supreme Court.

13

CONCEPT VOCABULARY

You will find the following terms and definitions useful as you read and discuss the selections in this book.

civil case court case that involves a dispute between individuals and organizations, in which compensation may be awarded to the victim

criminal case court case that involves a breach of state or federal law

double jeopardy putting a person on trial for an offense for which he or she has already been tried

due process a judicial requirement that enacted laws may not contain provisions that result in the unfair, arbitrary, or unreasonable treatment of an individual; also called *substantive due process*

grand jury a panel of citizens who decide whether it is appropriate for the government to prosecute someone suspected of a crime

incorporation doctrine the process by which American courts have applied the federal Bill of Rights to the states

probable cause facts or evidence that would make a reasonable person believe that a crime or wrongdoing has been, is being, or will be committed

procedural due process a course of formal proceedings carried out regularly and in accordance with established rules and principles, often used in reference to the lawful procedure of arresting and trying persons who have been accused of crimes

ratification process by which the Constitution was formally approved by the states

How Would Society Be Different

Without the First Amendment?

Thinking Skill EVALUATING ARGUMENTS

THE FIRST AMENDMENT

On June 7, 1789, Representative James Madison from Virginia introduced to the House of Representatives a list of amendments that he felt would "expressly declare the great rights of mankind secured under this constitution." Not all of them were adopted. Three of them were combined to form the First Amendment, which nearly 200 years later Supreme Court Justice Robert Jackson described as "a fixed star in our constitutional constellation."

Congress shall make no law respecting an establishment of religion, or prohibiting the free exercise thereof; or abridging the freedom of speech, or of the press; or the right of the people peaceably to assemble, and to petition the Government for a redress of grievances.

For many, the Bill of Rights is the most fundamental of the founding documents. "Protecting the rights of even the least individual among us," said President Ronald Reagan, "is basically the only excuse the government has for even existing."

George Washington and the Touro Synagogue

After Rhode Island ratified the Constitution—the last state to do so—Washington quickly made a trip there, stopping first at Newport. There, on August 18, 1790, Moses Seixas, warden of the Touro Synagogue, was one of many town and religious leaders to greet Washington and offer a welcoming address. Seixas's address seemed to ask for reassurance that Jews would have the right to worship freely in the new nation. President Washington promptly wrote a letter in reply, eloquently expressing the idea that religious freedom is not something that can be given by others but is instead a right born with each person. Following are excerpts from their exchange. Original spelling, punctuation, and capitalization have been retained.

Excerpts from the address of Moses Seixas

. . . With pleasure we reflect on those days ~~ those days of difficulty, and danger, when the God of Israel, who delivered David from the peril of the sword, ~~ shielded Your head in the day of battle. . . .

Deprived as we heretofore have been of the invaluable rights of free Citizens, we now with a deep sense of gratitude to the Almighty disposer of all events behold a Government, erected by the Majesty of the People ~~ a Government, which to bigotry gives no sanction, to persecution no assistance ~~ but generously affording to all Liberty of conscience, and immunities of Citizenship: ~~ deeming every one, of whatever Nation, tongue, or language equal parts of the great governmental Machine: ~~

For all these Blessings of civil and religious liberty which we enjoy under an equal benign[1] administration, we desire to send up our thanks to the Ancient of Days, the great preserver of Men ~~ beseeching[2] him, that the Angel who conducted our forefathers through the wilderness into the promised Land, may graciously conduct you through all the difficulties and dangers of this mortal life: ~~

---

1 **benign:** gentle, mild; favorable
2 **beseeching:** imploring; asking urgently

Excerpts from the reply from President Washington

. . . The reflection on the days of difficulty and danger which are past is rendered the more sweet, from a consciousness that they are succeeded by days of uncommon prosperity and security. If we have wisdom to make the best use of the advantages with which we are now favored, we cannot fail, under the just administration of a good Government, to become a great and happy people.

The Citizens of the United States of America have a right to applaud themselves for having given to mankind examples of an enlarged and liberal policy: a policy worthy of imitation. All possess alike liberty of conscience and immunities of citizenship. It is now no more that toleration is spoken of, as if it was by the indulgence of one class of people, that another enjoyed the exercise of their inherent natural rights. For happily the Government of the United States, which gives to bigotry no sanction, to persecution no assistance requires only that they who live under its protection should demean themselves as good citizens, in giving it on all occasions their effectual support. . . .

May the father of all mercies scatter light and not darkness in our paths, and make us all in our several vocations useful here, and in his own due time and way everlastingly happy.

Touro Synagogue is the oldest synagogue in America. Every year at the synagogue, the letter from Washington is read publicly.

Jefferson and the "Wall of Separation"

Even after the Bill of Rights was ratified in 1791, some minority religious groups worried that they were at the mercy of the majority because state laws did not prevent legislation related to religion. Baptists in Danbury, Connecticut were worried enough to write a letter in 1801 to President Thomas Jefferson expressing their concern that "what religious privileges we enjoy [as a minor part of the State] we enjoy as favors granted [by the Congregationalist majority], and not as inalienable rights." In his reply, Jefferson used a now-famous phrase: "a wall of separation between church and state."

Gentlemen,
The affectionate sentiments of esteem and approbation[1] which you are so good as to express towards me, on behalf of the Danbury Baptist Association, give me the highest satisfaction. . . .

Believing with you that religion is a matter which lies solely between man and his God, that he owes account to none other for his faith or his worship, that the legislative powers of government reach actions only, and not opinions, I contemplate with sovereign[2] reverence that act of the whole American people which declared that their legislature should "make no law respecting an establishment of religion, or prohibiting the free exercise thereof," thus building a wall of separation between church and State. Adhering[3] to this expression of the supreme will of the nation in behalf of the rights of conscience, I shall see with sincere satisfaction the progress of those sentiments which tend to restore to man all his natural rights, convinced he has no natural right in opposition to his social duties.

I reciprocate your kind prayers for the protection and blessing of the common Father and Creator of man, and tender[4] you for yourselves and your religious association, assurances of my high respect and esteem.

Thomas Jefferson
President of the United States

---

1   **approbation:** praise
2   **sovereign:** supreme
3   **Adhering:** Holding fast
4   **tender:** offer

Banning the Veil

Linda Chavez

In April of 2011, a law banning the wearing of full-face veils went into effect in France. Though broadly popular among the majority of French citizens, the ban has raised concern among Muslims in France, who protested in Paris and several other cities. American author and Fox News analyst Linda Chavez considers the relationship of this ban to religious freedom.

The French government this week decided to fine Muslim women who wear a full-face veil in public—and France is only the latest in a series of European countries seeking to ban the religious garb. Is this an infringement of religious liberty intended to discriminate against Muslims? Or is the measure necessary to protect the security of others? The answers are a lot more complicated than you might think.

A minority of Muslim women actually wear the burqa[1] or niqab[2] in Muslim countries or the West. The garb consists of a gown and headdress that covers the woman head to foot, revealing only her eyes. Obviously, it is impossible to determine who is under the veil—even whether the person is male or female. In Paris recently, a group of armed robbers pulled a heist wearing burqas, which made it not only impossible to identify them but easy for the criminals to conceal their weapons when entering the bank.

And the burqa presents even greater challenges when it comes to national security. Increasingly, we rely on cameras and facial recognition software to aid in protecting us against terrorism in public places. What's more, one of the most effective means for airport screeners to detect a potential terrorist is to assess the person's facial reactions: Does he or

---

1 **burqa:** A loose robe, usually with holes for the eyes, that covers the body from head to toe
2 **niqab:** A veil covering the hair and face with an opening for the eyes

she appear unduly furtive or nervous, for example. But these techniques are impossible if the person is wearing a burqa.

As Jean-François Copé, majority leader in the French National Assembly, wrote in a recent *New York Times* op-ed, "(The burqa) is not an article of clothing—it is a mask, a mask worn at all times, making identification or participation in economic and social life virtually impossible." And that is also its intent: to isolate the wearer from all aspects of public life.

As Copé notes in his op-ed, the Koran[3] does not tell women they must cover their face, and most Muslim women do not do so. The burqa goes far beyond protecting a woman's modesty; it transforms a woman into a non-person. She becomes a shrouded creature whose face and body are undistinguishable as a unique human being.

Two decades ago, it was exceedingly rare to see burqas in public in the United States. But, depending on where you live, burqas are now visible at shopping malls and on the street. What strikes me most when I encounter burqa-clad women is the contrast between their dress and their male companions'. Most of these women are covered in thick, black cloth, even in Washington's 90-plus degree summers, while the men wear short sleeves and light khakis.

Here's a challenge to Muslim men who believe that the wearing of the burqa is no hardship on women. Don one yourself and wear it for a week. Wear it to work and see if it impedes your ability to do your job. Wear it when you go out in public and see what it's like to try to interact with others. Wear it when you go to the local mall or the park or take your children for a walk. And, by all means, do so on the hottest day of the year.

The First Amendment would likely make a broad ban on the burqa in the United States unconstitutional, though some states have restricted its wearing for such activities as obtaining a driver's license. But it would be a false tolerance to suggest that we should treat the burqa as a symbol of religious freedom. The burqa is a statement about the woman's status more than a religious one. The burqa-clad woman is not an individual with rights; she belongs to a man—her husband, father or brothers— whose "property" must be protected from other men's gaze. We may not ban the burqa here, but we can and should disapprove of it.

---

3 **Koran:** Muslim holy book

DECLARATION OF CONSCIENCE

MARGARET CHASE SMITH

On June 1, 1950, Republican Senator Margaret Chase Smith (Maine) stood before her colleagues to speak out against the environment of suspicion that pervaded the government after Senator Joseph McCarthy (R., Wisconsin) announced his certainty that Communists were infiltrating the State Department. For four years Americans from many walks of life, including the army, were accused of being Communists, sometimes with ruinous results to their careers. After berating army witnesses in televised hearings in 1954, McCarthy was censured by the Senate. By 1957 the "Red Scare" began to subside.

Mr. President:

I would like to speak briefly and simply about a serious national condition. It is a national feeling of fear and frustration that could result in national suicide and the end of everything that we Americans hold dear. It is a condition that comes from the lack of effective leadership in either the Legislative Branch or the Executive Branch of our Government. . . .

The United States Senate has long enjoyed worldwide respect as the greatest deliberative body[1] in the world. But recently that deliberative character has too often been debased to the level of a forum of hate and character assassination sheltered by the shield of congressional immunity.[2]

It is ironical that we Senators can in debate in the Senate directly or indirectly, by any form of words impute[3] to any American, who is not a Senator, any conduct or motive unworthy or unbecoming an American—

---

1 **deliberative body:** group that reasons through issues with vigorous debate
2 **congressional immunity:** protection from arrest or prosecution for members of the House of Representatives and Senate while speaking on the floor, regardless of content, with certain extreme exceptions
3 **impute:** attribute; assign

and without that non-Senator American having any legal redress[4] against us—yet if we say the same thing in the Senate about our colleagues we can be stopped on the grounds of being out of order. . . .

I think that it is high time for the United States Senate and its members to do some soul searching—for us to weigh our consciences—on the manner in which we are performing our duty to the people of America—on the manner in which we are using or abusing our individual powers and privileges.

I think that it is high time that we remembered that we have sworn to uphold and defend the Constitution. I think that it is high time that we remembered that the Constitution, as amended, speaks not only of the freedom of speech but also of trial by jury instead of trial by accusation.

Whether it be a criminal prosecution in court or a character prosecution in the Senate, there is little practical distinction when the life of a person has been ruined.

Those of us who shout the loudest about Americanism in making character assassinations are all too frequently those who, by our own words and acts, ignore some of the basic principles of Americanism—
The right to criticize;
The right to hold unpopular beliefs;
The right to protest;
The right of independent thought.

The exercise of these rights should not cost one single American citizen his reputation or his right to a livelihood nor should he be in danger of losing his reputation or livelihood merely because he happens to know someone who holds unpopular beliefs. Who of us doesn't?

---

4 **redress:** remedy or compensation for a grievance

Otherwise none of us could call our souls our own. Otherwise thought control would have set in. . . .

As an American, I want to see our nation recapture the strength and unity it once had when we fought the enemy instead of ourselves.

It is with these thoughts I have drafted what I call a "Declaration of Conscience." *[Six other Republican senators joined her.]*

STATEMENT OF SEVEN REPUBLICAN SENATORS

1   We are Republicans. But we are Americans first. It is as Americans that we express our concern with the growing confusion that threatens the security and stability of our country. Democrats and Republicans alike have contributed to that confusion.

2   The Democratic administration has initially created the confusion by its lack of effective leadership, by its contradictory grave warnings and optimistic assurances, by its complacency[5] to the threat of communism here at home, by its oversensitiveness to rightful criticism, by its petty bitterness against its critics.

3   Certain elements of the Republican party have materially added to this confusion in the hopes of riding the Republican party to victory through the selfish political exploitation of fear, bigotry, ignorance, and intolerance. There are enough mistakes of the Democrats for Republicans to criticize constructively without resorting to political smears.

4   To this extent, Democrats and Republicans alike have unwittingly,[6] but undeniably, played directly into the Communist design of "confuse, divide, and conquer."

5   It is high time that we stopped thinking politically as Republicans and Democrats about elections and started thinking patriotically as Americans about national security based on individual freedom. It is high time that we all stopped being tools and victims of totalitarian techniques—techniques that, if continued here unchecked, will surely end what we have come to cherish as the American way of life.

---

5   **complacency:** a state of comfort and lack of awareness of a threat
6   **unwittingly:** unknowingly

Irregular Verbs

Aquiles Nazoa

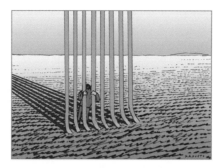

Despite the McCarthy era (see pages 24–26), some Americans may take their First Amendment rights for granted since they have been part of the nation's laws since 1791. However, even in modern times, free speech is not allowed in some parts of the world. Venezuelan journalist and writer Aquiles Nazoa always stood for the right of free expression, even during the turbulent times in the 1950s when a series of military coups threatened human liberties in Venezuela.

There are some verbs that are slow like a turtle
I conjugate
You conjugate
He conjugates

And since everyone is afraid with the lack of constitutional rights
I don't write
You don't write
He doesn't write

For if one writes all the thoughts under the veil
I go to jail
You go to jail
He goes to jail

—Translation by Vanessa Baird

Thoughts That We Hate

Anthony Lewis

In the 1929 Supreme Court case United States v. Schwimmer, *the court ruled 6–3 that citizenship could be denied to a woman from Hungary who refused to say she would take up arms to defend the United States—part of the oath of citizenship—because she was a Quaker and a pacifist. The Supreme Court reversed that ruling in a 1946 decision, allowing a Canadian citizen to become an American citizen even though he, too, was a pacifist—in his case on the strength of his beliefs as a Seventh-day Adventist. While the 1929 judgment crumbled, the words of dissenting Justice Oliver Wendell Holmes, Jr., have endured. He wrote, ". . . if there is any principle of the Constitution that more imperatively calls for attachment than any other it is the principle of free thought—not free thought for those who agree with us but freedom for the thought that we hate."*

It was in the case of a pacifist that Justice Holmes spoke of "freedom for the thought that we hate." But suppose it were not a pacifist but a Nazi. Would that change her right to freedom of expression? Should it?

Hate speech, it is called: virulent[1] attacks on Jews, blacks, Muslims, homosexuals, or members of any other group. It is pure hatred, not based on any wrong done by an individual. A German may have been a practicing Roman Catholic; but if the Nazis found that he had a Jewish grandfather, off he went to a death camp.

The United States differs from almost all other Western societies in its legal treatment of hate speech. In Germany it is a crime, a serious one, to display the swastika or any other Nazi symbol. In eleven European countries it is a crime to say that the Holocaust did not happen, that Germans in the Nazi years did not slaughter Jews. So it is in Canada, and the Canadian Supreme Court has decided that Holocaust deniers can be

---

1 **virulent:** poisonous and severe

prosecuted and punished despite that country's constitutional guarantee of free expression. In the United States, the First Amendment protects the right to deny the fact of the Holocaust.

At one point the Supreme Court took a different view of bans on hateful speech. In 1952, in the case of *Beauharnais v. Illinois,* it sustained an Illinois law that made it a crime to distribute any publication that "portrays depravity, criminality, unchastity or lack of virtue of a class of citizens, of any race, color, creed or religion," exposing them to contempt or being "productive of breach of the peace or riots." Joseph Beauharnais had distributed a leaflet urging Chicago authorities to stop the "invasion of white . . . neighborhoods and persons by the Negro."

Justice Frankfurter, writing the opinion for a 5–4 majority, saw the Illinois law as a group form of criminal libel[2]—which had existed in the American states from the beginning. "Illinois did not have to look beyond her own borders or await the tragic experience of the last three decades," Frankfurter said, "to conclude that willful purveyors of falsehood concerning racial and religious groups promote strife. . . ." He instanced the murder in 1837 of Elijah Parish Lovejoy, a newspaper editor in Alton, in southern Illinois, because he favored the abolition of slavery, and recent race riots in the Chicago area. "Libelous utterances," he said, were not "within the area of constitutionally protected speech." Justice Black, dissenting, said that the Illinois law was entirely different from statutes against libel of individuals, and much more subject to abuse. Any minority group that welcomed the decision, he said, should remember Pyrrhus's statement: "Another such victory and I am undone."[3]

The logical premise of Justice Frankfurter's Beauharnais opinion was undone by the 1964 decision in *New York Times v. Sullivan,* which ended the exclusion of libel from the protection of the First Amendment. Under Sullivan and cases stemming from it, public officials and public figures cannot recover damages for libel unless they can prove that a false statement of fact was published knowingly or recklessly. The generalized smear of hate speech—a Beauharnais pamphlet, for example—does not lend itself to the factual analysis contemplated by these later decisions,

---

2 **libel:** a false published statement that could hurt a person's reputation

3 **"Another such victory and I am undone."** King Pyrrhus of Epirus defeated the Romans at Heraclea in 280 BC and Asculum in 279 BC during the Pyrrhic War. Yet his army suffered such crippling losses that he said any more victories like that would bring his army to ruin. Justice Black was suggesting that the ruling might be used against minority groups.

however vicious the smear may have been. That was so, the Court indicated, even when the viciousness was directed at an individual, as in *Hustler* magazine's attack on Jerry Falwell.[4]

Moreover, the Court in 1969 put extremely tight restrictions on criminal punishment for speech attacking racial or religious groups [in] the case of *Brandenburg v. Ohio*. . . . The speaker there, a Ku Klux Klan leader, said, "Personally, I believe the [African American] should be returned to Africa, the Jew returned to Israel." The Supreme Court unanimously reversed his conviction because there was no proof that the speaker was inciting "imminent lawless action" or that such action was likely to occur.

The issue of free speech for Nazis is symbolized in American law by the word "Skokie." Skokie is a village near Chicago that in 1977 had a large Jewish population, including a substantial number who were survivors of Nazi concentration camps. An American Nazi party announced that it would hold a demonstration in Skokie, with the demonstrators wearing a swastika, the Hitler symbol. The village authorities passed ordinances that among other things prohibited the dissemination of anything, including signs and clothing, that "incites hatred against persons by reason of their race, national origin, or religion." The authorities also sought an injunction[5] to the same effect from the Illinois courts. Cases went through state and federal courts. The ultimate judgment was by the United States Court of Appeals for the Seventh Circuit, which held that the village ordinances designed to stop the demonstration were unconstitutional. The Nazi group then canceled its plan.

The Skokie episode created wide controversy among civil libertarians. Many members of the American Civil Liberties Union resigned because the ACLU had supported the Nazis' right to march. But the ACLU leadership did not budge, and in the end its stand probably improved its public standing and enlarged its membership.

Roger Errera, a French legal scholar and jurist, said that Europeans would not accept American tolerance for hateful speech, as in the Skokie case. The American view, he suggested, must be based on "an inveterate

---

4 ***Hustler* magazine's attack on Jerry Falwell:** *Hustler,* an adult magazine known for nudity and crude humor, parodied Jerry Falwell, a well-known conservative Southern Baptist televangelist. Falwell sued for damages, but in 1988 the Supreme Court ruled that public figures could not sue over parodies since they are understood not to be factual.

5 **injunction:** a judicial order to prevent or stop a course of action

This demonstration in north suburban Skokie was one of three in the Chicago area on July 4, 1977, protesting the Nazis' plan to march through the suburb, where many Holocaust survivors lived.

social and historical optimism"—which Europeans could not be expected to share after their tragic experience at the hands of the Nazis and Communists. Hitler had made his murderous intentions plain enough in *Mein Kampf*.[6] Wouldn't it have been better to imprison him for such expression before he could organize his words into horrendous reality?

That is the dominant view in Europe, but it is not the only one. *The Economist*, the British weekly with an orientation toward the United States, made strong arguments in 2006 against laws criminalizing Holocaust denial and other forms of racist speech. Such laws, it warned, could be interpreted to punish or restrain speech that "merely causes offense." It instanced the example of Oriana Fallaci, the great Italian journalist, who when she died in 2006 was awaiting trial for offending Islam in a critical essay about the religion. "The big danger," *The Economist* wrote, "is that, in the name of stopping bigots, one may end up by stopping all criticism."

A notorious English Holocaust-denier, David Irving, served thirteen months in an Austrian prison in 2006–2007 for speeches he made in that

---

6 *Mein Kampf: My Struggle,* a book by Adolf Hitler in which he mixed autobiography and exposition of his political views

country. Irving had sued an American author, Deborah Lipstadt, for libel for calling him a denier; an English judge, in a devastating judgment, found that the characterization was true. But Lipstadt said she regretted his imprisonment in Austria, which made him "a martyr to free speech."

The conflict over how to deal with hate speech grew more intense with the rise of Islamic extremism and terrorist acts at the beginning of the twenty-first century. Britain, one of several European countries with a substantial Muslim population, faced the issue particularly acutely. A number of imams[7] allegedly urged violent jihad[8] in sermons in their mosques. One was prosecuted and convicted for soliciting murder and racial hatred. A leader of a British Islamist group, Atilla Ahmet, said: "You are attacking our people in Muslim countries, in Iraq, in Afghanistan. So it's legitimate to attack British soldiers and policemen, government officials and even the White House." In July 2005 four Muslim suicide bombers killed fifty-two people in London subways and on a bus. A militant spokesman, Abu Izzadeen, called the bombings "praiseworthy." In 2007 he was arrested for a later speech and charged with encouraging terrorism.

The great statement of reasons for allowing even the most noxious[9] speech was made by [Supreme Court Justice Louis] Brandeis in his opinion in *Whitney v. California*: "Discussion affords ordinarily adequate protection against the dissemination of noxious doctrine," he wrote. And, "The fitting remedy for evil counsels is good ones." But even the Supreme Court's highly tolerant decision in *Brandenburg v. Ohio* in 1969 would allow legal action against speech that is intended to incite imminent lawlessness and is likely to do so. Doesn't a call for the murder of police and other officials pass that test, given the fact of actual murders in the Islamist cause? Given the context—an actual terrorist bombing in Britain—the Brandenburg requirement of imminence seems to me inappropriate.

One of the arguments for allowing hateful speech is that it makes the rest of us aware of terrible beliefs and strengthens our resolve to combat them. This argument was rudely countered by Jeremy Waldron, an Englishman who emigrated to teach law in the United States. He wrote:

---

7 **imam:** prayer leader of a mosque
8 **jihad:** in Islam, a religious obligation, a spiritual struggle, or a holy war
9 **noxious:** poisonous

> The costs of hate speech . . . are not spread evenly across the community that is supposed to tolerate them. The [racists] of the world may not harm the people who call for their toleration, but then few of them are depicted as animals in posters plastered around Leamington Spa [an English town].[10] We should speak to those who are depicted in this way, or those whose suffering or whose parents' suffering is mocked by the [Skokie neo-Nazis] before we conclude that tolerating this sort of speech builds character.

Something like Jeremy Waldron's view animated a movement, in the 1980s and 1990s, to ban hateful speech on university campuses. Spurred by members of minority groups, the movement aimed at racist speech. Proponents of banning hate speech against minorities said students who were victimized by such speech were traumatized by it. To deal with the problem, some professors and students called for the adoption of speech codes, with penalties for violations.

A significant number of universities adopted speech codes. In practice, they dealt with hurtful comments on a wide range of matters beyond the original proposal, race. One of the best-known codes, adopted by Stanford University, prohibited "harassment by personal vilification" when it was "intended to stigmatize an individual or a small number of individuals on the basis of their sex, race, color, handicap, religion, sexual orientation, or national and ethnic origin." A code proposed by the University of Massachusetts at Amherst in 1995 added to those subjects "age, marital status, veteran status." The graduate students' union there wanted to add "citizenship, culture, H.I.V status,[11] language, parental status, political belief and pregnancy."

The lengthening list of characteristics to be protected from harassing speech brought ridicule on the speech-code campaign. In 1989 a federal court held the University of Michigan code unconstitutional. Stanford's failed a legal test a few years later. And the campaign ebbed. . . .

The largest controversy about offensive speech in modern America concerned not a verbal utterance but symbolic expression: burning the flag. During the Republican National Convention in 1984 a group of

---

10 In the 1970s, a racist agitator plastered posters portraying Britons of African descent as apes. He was sentenced to a short prison term.

11 **H.I.V. status:** People with an H.I.V. positive status are infected with a virus that can lead to AIDS, a disease associated with homosexuals.

demonstrators marched through the streets protesting the policies of the Reagan administration. One of them, Gregory Lee Johnson, set an American flag on fire in front of the Dallas City Hall. He was convicted of violating a Texas law that prohibited desecration[12] of a "venerated[13] object." The Supreme Court, by a vote of 5 to 4, reversed his conviction, finding the flag-burning expressive conduct that was protected by the First Amendment. "If there is a bedrock principle underlying the First Amendment," Justice Brennan wrote in the opinion of the Court, "it is that the government may not prohibit the expression of an idea simply because society finds the idea itself offensive or disagreeable."

Many Americans indeed found the burning of the flag offensive. Congress came close to approving a constitutional amendment to allow the criminalizing of flag-burning. It did pass a criminal statute, the Flag Protection Act of 1989, to punish anyone who, except to dispose of a worn or soiled flag, "mutilates, defaces, physically defiles, burns, maintains on the floor or ground, or tramples upon any flag of the United States." In *United States v. Eichman* in 1990 the Supreme Court, by the identical 5–4 vote, held that statute unconstitutional. Justice Brennan, writing again for the majority, said the very list of prohibitions showed that the concern behind the act was "disrespectful treatment" of the flag. Thus the act "suppresses expression out of concern for its likely communicative impact." Justice Brennan concluded: "Punishing desecration of the flag dilutes the very freedom that makes this emblem so revered, and worth revering."

In the catalog of hateful or offensive expression, burning a flag is surely less dangerous than most other examples: anti-Semitic ravings in a Munich beer hall, say, or preaching to young Muslims in England that they should become suicide bombers. (One worshipper who heard such sermons, Richard Reid, tried unsuccessfully to blow up an airliner with a bomb in his shoe.)

In 1994 broadcasts on a radio station in Rwanda urged Hutus, who were a majority of the population, to kill Tutsis, the minority, and moderate-minded Hutus. A massacre followed, and more than 500,000 people were killed. Years later a Tutsi-led government forbade political parties to appeal to group identity, and public statements promoting "divisionism" were outlawed. Should we in America who have avoided

---

12 **desecration:** disrespecting
13 **venerated:** revered

such tragedies tell Rwandans that it is wrong for them thus to limit freedom of speech?

In an age when words have inspired acts of mass murder and terrorism, it is not as easy for me as it once was to believe that the only remedy for evil counsels, in Brandeis's phrase, should be good ones. The law of the American Constitution allows suppression only when violence or violation of law are intended by speakers and are likely to take place imminently. But perhaps judges, and the rest of us, will be more on guard now for the rare act of expression—not the burning of a flag or the racist slang of an undergraduate—that is genuinely dangerous. I think we should be able to punish speech that urges terrorist violence to an audience some of whose members are ready to act on the urging. That is imminence enough.

Louis D. Brandeis (1856-1941) served on the U.S. Supreme Court from 1916-1939. Stating his famous view about the remedy for bad ideas in more popular terms, he wrote, "Publicity is justly commended as a remedy for social and industrial diseases. Sunlight is said to be the best of disinfectants; electric light the most efficient policeman."

Are Violent Video Games Protected as Free Speech?

Not all speech is free. Over the years, the Supreme Court has determined that there are certain categories of speech unprotected by the First Amendment. These include "fighting words" (personal insults so strong that they would provoke a violent reaction), threats, advocacy of lawlessness, and obscenity. In November 2010, the Supreme Court heard oral arguments on whether violence in video games should be considered protected or unprotected speech. The case (Brown v. Entertainment Merchants Association) involved a California law that sought to limit the sale of violent video games to minors. A California court ruled that law unconstitutional, and the state of California (the Petitioners) appealed to the Supreme Court. The following excerpts from the transcript of the oral arguments show the tone of the proceedings and the ways in which the justices challenge claims to reach a decision.

ORAL ARGUMENT OF ZACKERY P. MORAZZINI ON BEHALF OF THE PETITIONERS November 2, 2010

MR. MORAZZINI: Mr. Chief Justice, and may it please the Court:

The California law at issue today before this Court differs from the New York law at issue in Ginsberg[1] in only one respect: Where New York was concerned with minors' access to harmful sexual material outside the guidance of a parent, California is no less concerned with a minor's access to the deviant level of violence that is presented in a certain category of video games that can be no less harmful to the development of minors.

When this Court in Ginsberg crafted a rule of law that permits States to regulate a minor's access to such material outside the presence of a parent, it did so for two fundamental reasons that are equally applicable

---

1 **Ginsberg:** The 1968 Supreme Court case *Ginsberg v. New York* in which the justices ruled that a state does have the right to protect the interests of minors and to limit their access to potentially harmful materials

this morning in this case. First, this rule permits parents' claim to authority in their own household to direct the upbringing and the development of their children; and, secondly, this rule promotes the States' independent interest in helping parents protect the well-being of children in those instances when parents cannot be present.

So this morning, California asks this Court to adopt a rule of law that permits States to restrict minors' ability to purchase deviant, violent video games that the legislature has determined can be harmful to the development and the upbringing --

JUSTICE (ANTONIN) SCALIA: What's a deviant -- a deviant, violent video game? As opposed to what? A normal violent video game?

MR. MORAZZINI: Yes, Your Honor. Deviant would be departing from established norms.

JUSTICE SCALIA: There are established norms of violence?

MR. MORAZZINI: Well, I think if we look back --

JUSTICE SCALIA: I mean, some of the Grimms' fairy tales are quite grim, to tell you the truth.

(Laughter.)

MR. MORAZZINI: Agreed, Your Honor. But the level of violence --

JUSTICE SCALIA: Are they okay? Are you going to ban them, too?

In the fairy tale "Hansel and Gretel" and in many others, the threat of grim violence runs through the story.

MR. MORAZZINI: Not at all, Your Honor.

JUSTICE (RUTH BADER) GINSBURG: What's the difference? mean, if you—if you are supposing a category of violent materials dangerous to children, then how do you cut it off at video games? What about films? What about comic books? Grimms' fairy tales? Why are video games special? Or does your principle extend to all deviant, violent materials in whatever form?

MR. MORAZZINI: No, Your Honor. That's why I believe California incorporated the three prongs of the Miller standard.[2] So it's not just deviant violence. It's not just patently offensive violence. It's violence that meets all three of the terms set forth in --

CHIEF JUSTICE (JOHN) ROBERTS: I think that misses Justice Ginsburg's question, which was: Why just video games? Why not movies, for example, as well?

MR. MORAZZINI: Sure, Your Honor. The California Legislature was presented with substantial evidence that demonstrates that the interactive nature of violent -- of violent video games where the minor or the young adult is the aggressor, is the -- is the individual acting out this -- this obscene level of violence, if you will, is especially harmful to minors. It --

JUSTICE (ELENA) KAGAN: Well, do you actually have studies that show that video games are more harmful to minors than movies are?

MR. MORAZZINI: Well, in the record, Your Honor, I believe it's the Gentile and Gentile study[3] regarding violent video games as exemplary teachers. The authors there note that video games are not only exemplary teachers of pro-social activities, but also exemplary teachers of aggression, which was the fundamental concern of the California Legislature in enacting this statute.

---

2 **Miller standard:** The test established in the 1973 Supreme Court case *Miller v. California* to determine if a work is obscene. The three prongs of the test are: 1) the average person applying contemporary community standards would find that the work appealed to baser interests; 2) that subject matter is presented in a clearly offensive way; and 3) that the work has no serious literary or artistic value.

3 **Gentile and Gentile study:** Gentile, D. A. & Gentile, J. R. (2008). Violent video games as exemplary teachers: A conceptual analysis. *Journal of Youth and Adolescence*, 9, 127-141.

So, while the science is continually developing—indeed, it appears that studies are being released every month regarding --

CHIEF JUSTICE ROBERTS: What was the --

JUSTICE KAGAN: And suppose -- suppose a new study suggested that movies were just as violent. Then, presumably, California could regulate movies just as it could regulate video games.

MR. MORAZZINI: Well, Your Honor, there is scientific literature out there regarding the impact of violent media on -- on children. In fact, for decades, the President, Congress, the FTC,[4] parenting groups have been uniquely concerned with the level of violent media available to minors that they have ready access to. So --

JUSTICE (SONIA) SOTOMAYOR: I don't know—is that answering Justice Kagan's question? One of the studies, the Anderson study,[5] says that the effect of violence is the same for a Bugs Bunny episode as it is for a violent video. So can the legislature now, because it has that study, say we can outlaw Bugs Bunny?

MR. MORAZZINI: No --

JUSTICE SOTOMAYOR: And there are people who would say that the cartoon has very little social value; it's entertainment but not much else. This is entertainment. I'm not suggesting that I like this video, the one at issue that you provided the five-minute clip about. To me, it's not entertainment, but that's not the point. To some, it may well be.

MR. MORAZZINI: Justice Sotomayor, cartoons do not depart from the established norms to -- of a level of violence to which children have been historically exposed to. We believe the level of violence in these video games --

JUSTICE SCALIA: That same argument could have been made when movies first came out. They could have said, oh, we've had violence in

---

4 **FTC:** Federal Trade Commission
5 **Anderson study:** Research by Dr. Craig Anderson, psychology professor, Iowa State University

Grimms' fairy tales, but we've never had it, you know, live on the screen. I mean, every time there's a new technology, you can make that argument.

MR. MORAZZINI: Well, Your Honor, I think that's the beauty of incorporating the three prongs of the Miller standard into California's law. This standard is very prophylactic[6] and ensures that only a narrow category of material will be covered, certainly not Grimms' fairy tales.

JUSTICE SOTOMAYOR: How is this any different than what we said we don't do in the First Amendment field in Stevens,[7] where we said we don't look at a category of speech and decide that some of it has low value. We decide whether a category of speech has a historical tradition of being regulated. Now, other than some State statutes that you point to, some of which are very clearly the same as those that we struck down in Wynn,[8] where's the tradition of regulating violence?

[After hearing more arguments from the State of California, the judges turned their attention to the arguments of the video game industry (the Respondents), represented in court by attorney Paul M. Smith.]

MR. SMITH: Mr. Chief Justice, and may it please the Court:

The California law at issue restricts the distribution of expressive works based on their content. California, as we've heard today, does not seriously contend that it can satisfy the usual First Amendment standards that apply to such a law. Instead, it's asking this Court to grant it a new free pass, a brand-new Ginsberg-like exception to the First Amendment that would deny constitutional protection to some ill-defined subset of expressive works and, I submit, not just video games, but necessarily movies, books, and any other expressive work that describes or portrays violence in a way that some court somewhere, some day, would decide is deviant and offensive.

---

6 **prophylactic:** preventive
7 **Stevens:** The 2010 Supreme Court case *United States v. Stevens* in which the judges ruled that a law prohibiting the sale of videos of animal cruelty, such as dogfights, violated First Amendment rights
8 **Wynn:** The 2009 Supreme Court case *United States v. Wynn* in which the judges considered whether the crime committed by Antonio Wynn qualified as a "crime of violence" and therefore should be considered in his sentencing

CHIEF JUSTICE ROBERTS: What about -- the distinction between books and movies may be that, in these video games, the child is not sitting there passively watching something; the child is doing the killing. The child is doing the maiming. And I suppose that might be understood to have a different impact on the child's moral development.

MR. SMITH: Well, Your Honor, it might. The -- the State of California has not marshaled a shred of evidence to suggest it's true. And if you look at the social science --

CHIEF JUSTICE ROBERTS: What was -- what was the state of the record that was present before the Court in Ginsberg?

MR. SMITH: The state of the record was that they were aware of science on both sides, but made a judgment that as a matter of common sense, they could decide that obscenity, even somewhat at-large obscenity --

CHIEF JUSTICE ROBERTS: So the Court acted on the basis of common sense?

MR. SMITH: Yes. It said as long as there's science on both sides, but in that particular area, which is an exception based -- that goes back to the founding, they felt that it was -- it was proper for them to adjust the outer boundaries of the exception. . . .

JUSTICE (SAMUEL) ALITO: You seem to argue that -- that there really is no good reason to think that exposure to video games is -- is bad for minors, exposure to really violent video games is bad to minors; is that right?

MR. SMITH: I think it's important to draw a distinction between harm that could be cognizable[9] under the law and appropriateness. Families have different judgments that they make about their children at different ages and with different content and different family values, and that's what --

JUSTICE KAGAN: Well, Mr. Smith, is there any showing that the State could make that would satisfy you, that would say, yes, that's a sufficient showing for this law to go forward?

---

9 **cognizable:** clearly identifiable

You know, I understand that you think that the current studies don't suggest much of anything about harm.

MR. SMITH: No, they don't.

JUSTICE KAGAN: But -- but are there studies that would be enough?

MR. SMITH: Well, I guess I can imagine a world in which expression could transform 75 percent of the people who experience it into murderers. That's clearly not the way the human mind works. And here the reality is quite the opposite. Dr. Anderson testified in the Illinois trial, which is in the record, that the vast majority of people playing the games will grow up and be just fine. And, in fact, he -- he acknowledged that the effects of these games are not one whit different from watching cartoons on television or reading violent passages in the Bible or looking at a picture of a gun.

JUSTICE ALITO: So why --

JUSTICE SCALIA: But you really don't want to argue the case on that ground. I -- I gather you don't believe that the First Amendment reads: Congress shall make no law abridging the freedom of speech except those that make sense. Is that --

MR. SMITH: Your Honor, my main ground today is exactly that, that this Court said last year in *United States v. Stevens* it doesn't have a freewheeling authority to create new exceptions to the First Amendment after 200 years based on a cost-benefit analysis, and this is -- this is a test of that. This is exactly what the State of California is asking you to do.

JUSTICE ALITO: But we have here a new -- a new medium that cannot possibly have been envisioned at the time when the First Amendment was ratified. It is totally different from -- it's one thing to read a description of -- as one of these -- one of these video games is promoted as saying, "What's black and white and red all over? Perhaps the answer could include disposing of your enemies in a meat grinder." Now, reading that is one thing. Seeing it as graphically portrayed --

JUSTICE SCALIA: And doing it.

JUSTICE ALITO: -- and doing it is still a third thing. So this presents a question that could not have been specifically contemplated at the time when the First Amendment was adopted. And to say, well, because nobody was -- because descriptions in a book of violence were not considered a category of speech that was appropriate for limitation at the time when the First Amendment was violated is entirely artificial.

MR. SMITH: We do have a new medium here, Your Honor, but we have a history in this country of new mediums coming along and people vastly overreacting to them, thinking the sky is falling, our children are all going to be turned into criminals. It started with the crime novels of the late 19th century, which produced

Dragon slayers are not just characters in modern video games. In this scene from the Anglo-Saxon epic poem, Beowulf battles a fire-breathing dragon. He is the first dragon slayer ever mentioned in English literature.

this raft of legislation which was never enforced. It started with comic books and movies in the 1950s. There were hearings across the street in the 1950s where social scientists came in and intoned to the Senate that half the juvenile delinquency in this country was being caused by reading comic books, and there was enormous pressure on the industry. They censored -- they self-censored. We have television. We have rock lyrics. We have the Internet. . . .

MR. SMITH: Let me -- I think a little history is helpful here. This Court has twice dealt with laws attempting to regulate violent works in the past. One was in *Winters v. New York*, where law applied to magazines and books, and one was in the 1960s. On the very day Ginsberg came down, in the Interstate Circuit case, the City of Dallas had an ordinance where there was going to be a commission that was going to review each movie and decide if it was appropriate for children.

JUSTICE ALITO: Let me be clear about exactly what your argument is. Your argument is that there is nothing that a State can do to limit minors' access to the most violent, sadistic, graphic video game that can be developed. That's your argument?

MR. SMITH: My position is --

JUSTICE ALITO: Is it or isn't it?

MR. SMITH: My position is that strict scrutiny applies, and that given the facts in the record, given the fact that the -- the problem is already well controlled, the parents are already empowered, and there are greatly less alternatives out there --

JUSTICE SOTOMAYOR: So, when you --

MR. SMITH: -- there isn't any basis to say scrutiny is satisfied.

JUSTICE SOTOMAYOR: So, when you say that --

CHIEF JUSTICE ROBERTS: So, just to be clear, your answer to Justice Alito is, at this point, there is nothing the State can do?

MR. SMITH: Because there's no problem it needs to solve that would justify --

CHIEF JUSTICE ROBERTS: Could I -- could I just have a simple answer?

MR. SMITH: The answer is yes, Your Honor.

CHIEF JUSTICE ROBERTS: There's nothing the State can do.

JUSTICE SOTOMAYOR: Mr. Smith, how can you say that? There's plenty of proof that -- that children are going into stores and buying these games despite the voluntary rating system, despite the voluntary retailer restraint by some. There's still proof out there, and an abundance of it, that kids are buying the games.

MR. SMITH: I disagree.

JUSTICE SOTOMAYOR: And there's proof that some parents, as well-intentioned as they may or may not be, have not been able to supervise that. So I -- starting from the proposition that there is a problem, it's a compelling State need, why are you arguing that there is no solution that the State could use to address that problem?

MR. SMITH: The -- the existing solutions are perfectly capable of allowing this problem to be addressed, assuming it is a problem. And I would --

JUSTICE SOTOMAYOR: But it's still about 20 percent of sales are going to kids.

MR. SMITH: That's when they send in somebody who's 16 to test the system. There isn't any evidence at all in this record that actual children, not testers, are in fact disobeying their parents and secretly buying these games, bringing them into the home, and playing them for years with their parents unaware of it. There's simply no evidence of that at all.

CHIEF JUSTICE ROBERTS: Could you have a law that says the State has to put -- the dealers have to put the violent video games in a particular area of the video store?

MR. SMITH: There -- there is --

CHIEF JUSTICE ROBERTS: That is not -- and then -- you know, and minors are not allowed in that area.

MR. SMITH: Well, if what you're saying is you're going to have a limit on the ability of minors to buy them because of walled off, and minors are not allowed --

CHIEF JUSTICE ROBERTS: Yes.

MR. SMITH: -- to go pick them off the shelf, then I don't know how that differs from the current law, Your Honor, assuming you could figure out --

JUSTICE (STEPHEN) BREYER: Your answer -- your answer to the first question of Justice Alito and the Chief Justice was yes, isn't that -- that you are saying there's nothing they can do. So now, am I right about that or am I not right?

MR. SMITH: Yes. Strict scrutiny does not make sense --

JUSTICE BREYER: I am right? Okay. All I wanted was an answer to that.

CHIEF JUSTICE ROBERTS: So they can't say, example, all the -- all the highest rated videos have to be on the top shelf out of the reach of children. Can they do that?

MR. SMITH: I would think that that's probably not --

CHIEF JUSTICE ROBERTS: That's what they do with cigarettes or something, isn't it?

MR. SMITH: Except that cigarettes are not speech, Your Honor. This is fully protected speech.

CHIEF JUSTICE ROBERTS: I know that cigarettes are not speech, Mr. Smith.

(Laughter.)

CHIEF JUSTICE ROBERTS: Cigarettes are something that we have determined are harmful to children. The question is, you say the record doesn't support the idea that these video games are harmful to children. Some of us may conclude that it does.

MR. SMITH: Well, surely the record doesn't support it. The record says that if -- even if you take the studies at face value, it's not one whit more harmful than watching television cartoons. That's what the record shows. . . .

* * * * * * * * * * * * * * * * *

[Following the Respondents' argument, the Petitioners have a chance at rebuttal.]

JUSTICE KAGAN: Do you think *Mortal Kombat* is prohibited by this statute?

MR. MORAZZINI: I believe it's a candidate, Your Honor, but I haven't played the game and been exposed to it sufficiently to judge for myself.

JUSTICE KAGAN: It's a candidate, meaning, you know, yes, a reasonable jury could find that Mortal Kombat—which is, you know, an iconic game, which I'm sure half of the clerks who work for us spent considerable amounts of time in their adolescence playing.

(Laughter.)

MR. MORAZZINI: Justice Kagan --

JUSTICE SCALIA: I don't know what she's talking about.

(Laughter.)

MR. MORAZZINI: Justice Kagan, by "candidate," I meant that the video game industry should look at it, should take a long look at it. Now -- but I don't know off the top of my head. I'm willing to state right here in open court that the video game *Postal 2*, yes, would be covered by this Act. I'm willing to guess that games we described in our brief, such as *MadWorld*, would be covered by the Act. I think the video game industry --

JUSTICE SOTOMAYOR: Would a video game that portrayed a Vulcan, as opposed to a human being, being maimed and tortured -- would that be covered by the Act?

MR. MORAZZINI: No, it wouldn't, Your Honor, because the Act is only directed towards the range of options that are able to be inflicted on a human being.

* * * * * * * * * * * * * * * * *

[On June 27, 2011, the Court handed down its ruling, 7-2.]

Like the protected books, plays, and movies that preceded them, video games communicate ideas—and even social messages—through many familiar literary devices (such as characters, dialogue, plot, and music) and through features distinctive to the medium (such as the player's interaction with the virtual world). That suffices to confer First Amendment protection.

RESPONDING TO CLUSTER ONE

How Would Society Be Different Without the First Amendment?

Critical Thinking Skill EVALUATING ARGUMENTS

1. Evaluate the reasons Jefferson gives for holding in "sovereign reverence" the clause in the First Amendment that guarantees religious freedom. Identify each supporting point as fact, opinion, or reasoned judgment.

2. In "Banning the Veil," Linda Chavez says: "We may not ban the burqa here, but we can and should disapprove of it." Trace the claims Chavez makes to support that view and evaluate the reasoning behind each claim.

3. By what reasoning does Margaret Chase Smith conclude that by establishing a climate of suspicion, Democrats and Republicans were threatening "the American way of life"?

4. Using details from "Thoughts That We Hate," summarize the reasons people have for supporting bans on hate speech, as well as the reasons people have for opposing such bans. Create and complete a chart similar to the one below to help you gather and organize the various reasons. Then evaluate those reasons, explaining which seem most persuasive.

Reasons for supporting bans on hate speech	Reasons for opposing bans on hate speech

5. Closely read the arguments put forward by the Petitioners and those put forward by the Respondents in the transcript of oral arguments on First Amendment protection of violent video games. Analyze how each side refers to previous court cases to support its claims.

Writing Activity: Evaluate an Argument

Analyze the selections in this cluster, looking for information, claims, and evidence that have a bearing on the issue of the rights of the Nazis to march in Skokie. Then closely read the arguments Anthony Lewis lays out on that topic in the selection "Thoughts That We Hate." Evaluate the arguments the courts made on the Skokie march. You might present your evaluation in a chart or discuss it in an essay.

A Strong Evaluation

- evaluates the argument's premises by corroborating or challenging them with other information
- evaluates the argument's claims to decide whether they follow logically from the premises
- evaluates the argument's evidence by corroborating or challenging it with other information

CLUSTER TWO

How Well Does Federalism
Protect Individual Rights?

Thinking Skill DEFINING KEY WORDS AND PHRASES

THE SPIRIT OF LIBERTY

JUDGE LEARNED HAND

On May 21, 1944, while World War II raged, thousands of new American citizens gathered in Central Park, New York City, to celebrate "I Am an American Day," a holiday now observed in mid-September as "Constitution Day and Citizenship Day." Addressing the throngs who had just obtained their citizenship, Judge Learned Hand eloquently expressed the values that continue to draw so many to the land.

We have gathered here to affirm a faith, a faith in a common purpose, a common conviction, a common devotion. Some of us have chosen America as the land of our adoption; the rest have come from those who did the same. For this reason we have some right to consider ourselves a picked group, a group of those who had the courage to break from the past and brave the dangers and the loneliness of a strange land. What was the object that nerved us, or those who went before us, to this choice? We sought liberty; freedom from oppression, freedom from want, freedom to be ourselves. This we then sought; this we now believe that we are by way of winning. What do we mean when we say that first of all we seek liberty? I often wonder whether we do not rest our hopes too much upon constitutions, upon laws and upon courts. These are false hopes; believe me, these are false hopes. Liberty lies in the hearts of men and women; when it dies there, no constitution, no law, no court can even do much to help it. While it lies there it needs no constitution, no law, no court to save it. And what is this liberty which must lie in the hearts of men and women? It is not the ruthless, the unbridled will; it is not freedom to do as one likes. That is the denial of liberty, and leads straight to its overthrow. A society in which men recognize no check upon their freedom soon becomes a society where freedom is the possession of only a savage few; as we have learned to our sorrow.

What then is the spirit of liberty? I cannot define it; I can only tell you my own faith. The spirit of liberty is the spirit which is not too sure that it is right; the spirit of liberty is the spirit which seeks to understand the mind of other men and women; the spirit of liberty is the spirit which weighs their interests alongside its own without bias; the spirit of liberty remembers that not even a sparrow falls to earth unheeded; the spirit of liberty is the spirit of Him who, near two thousand years ago, taught mankind that lesson it has never learned but never quite forgotten; that there may be a kingdom where the least shall be heard and considered side by side with the greatest. And now in that spirit, that spirit of an America which has never been, and which may never be; nay, which never will be except as the conscience and courage of Americans create it; yet in the spirit of that America which lies hidden in some form in the aspirations of us all; in the spirit of that America for which our young men are at this moment fighting and dying; in that spirit of liberty and of America I ask you to rise and with me pledge our faith in the glorious destiny of our beloved country.

I pledge allegiance to the flag of the United States of America and to the republic for which it stands—One nation, Indivisible, with liberty and justice for all.

Since 2011, between 600,000 and 1,100,000 people have become new American citizens each year, often in mass naturalization events like the one pictured here.

THE DOLL TEST AND THE FOURTEENTH AMENDMENT

NAT HENTOFF

Although the Bill of Rights consists of only the first ten amendments to the Constitution, the issue of individual rights cannot be properly considered without recognizing the vital role of the Fourteenth Amendment in ensuring that some rights protected by the federal government must also be protected by state governments. (See pages 11–13.) The 1954 landmark Supreme Court decision in Brown v. Board of Education of Topeka, *which struck down the concept of "separate but equal" schools for blacks and whites, relied on the equal protection clause of the Fourteenth Amendment. That clause declares that no state can "deny to any person within its jurisdiction the equal protection of the laws." In the selection that follows, the writer chronicles the work of two African American psychologists whose research helped convince the court that separate facilities for blacks and whites had devastating effects.*

When Mamie Clark was working toward her master's degree, she did her fieldwork among schoolchildren in Washington, D.C. She was studying the effects of race on the way the children felt about themselves. Kenneth Clark also became absorbed in the work, and together they broadened the field of research and began publishing pioneering studies in various social-science journals on how segregation affected preschool black children's sense of self-esteem. Today, when the results of such studies are taken for granted, it's hard to imagine a time when there was a need for such studies. In one series of tests, administered to children between the ages of three and seven in, among other places, Philadelphia, Boston, Worcester, [MA,] and several cities in Arkansas, the children were asked to choose between otherwise identical brown and white dolls in response to such instructions as these:

Give me the doll that you like to play with.
Give me the doll that is the nice doll.
Give me the doll that looks bad.
Give me the doll that is a nice color.

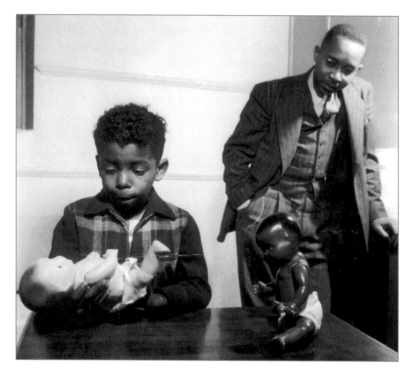

The Clarks reported that the majority of the children "indicated an unmistakable preference for the white doll and a rejection of the brown doll." They concluded, "The fact that young Negro children would prefer to be white reflects their knowledge that society prefers white people."

In 1950 Clark wrote a monograph[1] for the Midcentury White House Conference on Children and Youth, in which he summarized not only his and his wife's research but also the rest of the existing literature on the effects of racial segregation on black children. The monograph came to the attention of Robert Carter, a young lawyer with the National Association for the Advancement of Colored People.

---

1 **monograph:** detailed study on a specialized topic

An NAACP legal team, headed by Thurgood Marshall,[2] decided to make an all-out attack on the constitutionality of state laws mandating[3] or permitting segregation of the schools. Such statutes, NAACP claimed, violated the equal-protection clause of the Fourteenth Amendment ("No state shall . . . deny to any person within its jurisdiction the equal protection of the laws"). Carter thought that Clark might be a useful witness in some of the pending cases; he also wanted to explore with Clark the possibility of enlisting other social scientists to buttress the NAACP argument that "separate but equal" schooling not only was inherently unequal but inflicted psychological damage on the segregated black children.

The "separate but equal" doctrine had been established by the Supreme Court in *Plessy v. Ferguson* (1896). During a train trip in Louisiana, Homer Plessy, a "seven-eighths Caucasian"—he had had one Negro great-grandparent—refused to move to a car for "colored" passengers, as a recently passed state law required. A New Orleans judge ruled that, contrary to Plessy's argument, the segregation statute did not violate the Fourteenth Amendment. On appeal, the Supreme Court, by a seven-to-one vote, affirmed the lower court's decision. Justice Henry Billings Brown, speaking for the majority, declared that laws requiring racial separation "do not necessarily imply the inferiority of either race to the other." Indeed, he said, "we consider the underlying fallacy[4] of the plaintiff's argument to consist in the assumption that the enforced separation of the two races stamps the colored race with a badge of inferiority."

He continued, "If this be so, it is not by reason of anything found in the act, but solely because the colored race chooses to put that construction upon it." As long as they were equal, separate facilities, based on "the established usages, customs, and traditions of the people," were constitutional. And to give further support to that conclusion, Justice Brown noted that "the most common instance" of lawful segregation "is connected with the establishment of separate schools for white and colored children, which have been held to be a valid exercise of the legislative power even by courts of states where the political rights of the colored race have been longest and most earnestly enforced."

---

2 **Thurgood Marshall:** Marshall became the first African American Supreme Court Justice in 1967. Before that, he had argued more cases before the Supreme Court than anyone else in history.

3 **mandating:** requiring

4 **fallacy:** unsound reasoning

In 1951, when the NAACP was organizing its legal strategy for getting *Plessy* overturned, racial segregation of children was in force in more than eleven thousand school districts in the United States. (Seventeen states and the District of Columbia had passed laws establishing school segregation, and four other states allowed school segregation where it was the wish of a local community.) . . .

One approach to combating racial separation in elementary and secondary schools was to keep bringing lawsuits on the basis that a particular black educational facility was unequal to its white counterpart. Because this was indeed the case in most segregated school districts, the NAACP figured that it could win discrete[5] victories on these grounds; however, to break down the racial walls on a case-by-case basis might take a half century or more. The alternative was to launch a direct assault on the *Plessy* doctrine by arguing that even if all facilities were "equal," the very nature of segregation made separate education profoundly unequal for black children and profoundly damaging to their sense of self-worth.

In February 1951, Kenneth Clark began to work with NAACP lawyers on the preparation of three of the four cases—from Kansas, South Carolina, Virginia, and Delaware—that, three years later, were to be grouped by the Supreme Court in its *Brown v. Board of Education* decision. In all but the Kansas suit (the title case), Clark testified and helped recruit other social scientists as witnesses. The NAACP had used social-science testimony before. In *Sweatt,*[6] for instance, an anthropologist had testified on scientific interpretation of racial differences. But now the legal strategy was to include a systematic analysis—by psychologists, sociologists, anthropologists, and a variety of experts on education—of the nature of segregation itself and of its effects on children.

As a witness in one of the four test cases, *Briggs v. Elliott,* Clark testified before the federal district court in Charleston, South Carolina, in May 1951, saying the following:

> I have reached the conclusion from the examination of my own results and from an examination of the literature in the entire field that discrimination, prejudice, and segregation have definitely detrimental[7] effects on the personality development of

---

5 **discrete:** separate; distinct
6 **Sweatt:** *Sweatt v. Painter,* a 1950 Supreme Court case ruled in favor of a black applicant who had been denied admission to a Texas law school because the state forbade integrated education
7 **detrimental:** harmful

the Negro child. The essence of this detrimental effect is a confusion in the child's concept of his own self-esteem—basic feelings of inferiority, conflict, confusion in his self-image, resentment, hostility toward himself, hostility toward whites, intensification of . . . a desire to resolve his basic conflict by sometimes escaping or withdrawing.

On May 17, 1954, the Court, in a unanimous decision delivered by Chief Justice Earl Warren, overturned *Plessy v. Ferguson.* To separate black children "from others of similar age and qualifications solely because of their race generates a feeling of inferiority as to their status in the community that may affect their hearts and minds in a way unlikely ever to be undone," the Court declared. "Whatever may have been the extent of psychological knowledge at the time of *Plessy v. Ferguson,* this finding is amply supported by modern authority." At that point in the decision, there was a footnote, No. 11, consisting of a list of sources exemplifying "modern authority," the first of which was "K. B. Clark, 'Effect of Prejudice and Discrimination on Personality Development' (Midcentury White House Conference on Children and Youth, 1950)." The Court continued: "We conclude that in the field of public education the doctrine of 'separate but equal' has no place. Separate educational facilities are inherently unequal. Therefore, we hold that the plaintiffs and others similarly situated for whom the actions have been brought are, by reason of the segregation complained of, deprived of the equal protection of the laws guaranteed by the Fourteenth Amendment."

Kenneth Clark was, of course, jubilant—the more so because it appeared that the Supreme Court had taken "judicial notice," as he put it, of that unusual social-science appendix. As his professors at Howard University had taught him, disciplined intelligence could achieve social justice, and the social sciences were surely going to be as effective in their fields as the biological sciences were in theirs.

Despite the unanimity of the Supreme Court in *Brown,* and despite its acknowledgment of "modern authority," racism has, of course, proved much more intransigent[8] than Clark anticipated in the immediate aftermath of the striking down of *Plessy.* But long after it had become clear that the expectations of that May day might not be fulfilled until the end of the century—if then—Dr. Clark was still emphasizing the historic impact of the 1954 decision. In 1976, delivering a speech in Munich

---

8 **intransigent:** hard to change; unyielding

titled "The Status of American Minorities in the Bicentennial Year of the American Revolution," he noted:

> Within three years after the *Brown* decision, Martin Luther King Jr., Roy Wilkins, Whitney Young, and Malcolm X emerged as the significant leaders of the modern civil-rights movement, which then became in effect a mass movement. American . . . blacks who seemed to have accepted compliantly[9] racial segregation since the latter part of the nineteenth century now openly defied institutionalized racism. They refused to sit in the back of the bus. They boycotted all public accommodations that sought to impose racial humiliation upon them.

And in the wake of *Brown,* Clark added, Congress passed the Civil Rights Act of 1964 and the Voting Rights Act of 1965.

That said, Clark, in his bicentennial lecture, turned to the distinction between appearance and substance. After all the marches, demonstrations, and new laws, the majority of blacks "are still to be found in menial positions, are underemployed, or unemployed," he pointed out. "Most black children, twenty-two years after the *Brown* decision, are still required by various evasive devices to attend racially segregated and inferior schools." He continued:

> This problem is particularly exacerbated[10] in northern urban communities, such as Boston, New York, Chicago, Philadelphia, Los Angeles. These so-called cosmopolitan centers of America are now the bastions[11] of sustained resistance to . . . the desegregation of their schools. Racially segregated communities remain the norm in American cities. White suburbs remain predominantly white *Bantustans,*[12] with only occasional Negroes being permitted to purchase homes within these compounds of privilege. Urban ghettos are expanding and proliferating, and the pathologies of the ghettos—crime, drugs, defeatism of the young, reinforced by inferior education—remain unsolved problems which threaten the viability if not the survival of major American cities.

---

9 **compliantly:** agreeing to established rules

10 **exacerbated:** made worse

11 **bastions:** fortresses

12 **Bantustans:** homelands set aside for Black South Africans under the apartheid system of racial segregation

Brown had indeed made history, but not enough.

In the decades since *Brown,* Kenneth Clark has become more and more firmly convinced that the primary way to regenerate the hopes and energies ignited by the *Brown* decision is to transform the schools. In speeches and seminars, he has repeated this theme: "One cannot expect a group to attain the full status of equality of citizenship if the masses of the children of that group are being denied adequate education in their elementary and secondary schools, if the abilities of these children are not being developed to the maximum at these crucial stages of their development, and if these children are being subjected to educational experiences which deprive them of the ability to compete successfully with others."

To prevent nine African American students from enrolling at Little Rock Central High following the *Brown v. Board of Education* ruling, Governor Orval Faubus of Arkansas ordered the Arkansas National Guard to block their entrance. President Dwight D. Eisenhower responded by nationalizing the Arkansas militia and sending federal troops (above) to protect the students and make sure they were able to attend. The students have become known as the "Little Rock Nine," and their story was a major event in the movement toward civil rights for African Americans.

THE COURAGE OF THEIR CONVICTIONS: FANNIE LOU HAMER

LINDA R. MONK

The Fifteenth Amendment addressing voting rights has also played a key role in assuring that states do not take away individual rights. It says: "The right of citizens of the United States to vote shall not be denied or abridged by the United States or by any State on account of race, color, or previous condition of servitude." In the selection that follows, the writer shows how—even long after the passage of the Fifteenth Amendment in 1870—voting rights had to be hard won.

The youngest of twenty children of Mississippi sharecroppers, Fannie Lou Hamer (1917–1977) became a national leader of the civil rights movement. Her motto was, "I'm sick and tired of being sick and tired." In her autobiography, *To Praise Our Bridges,* Fannie Lou Hamer described when, at the age of 44, she first tried to register to vote:

> I . . . stayed on the plantation until 1962, when I went down to the courthouse in Indianola to register to vote. That happened because I went to a mass meeting one night. Until then I'd never heard of no mass meeting and I didn't know that a Negro could register and vote. . . . When [the civil rights workers] asked for those to raise their hands who'd go down to the courthouse the next day, I raised mine. Had it up high as I could get it. I guess if I'd had any sense I'd a-been a little scared, but what was the point of being scared. The only thing they could do to me was kill me and it seemed like they'd been trying to do that a little bit at a time ever since I could remember.

When she tried to register to vote, Fannie Lou Hamer was forced to take a literacy test, in which she had to explain one of the 286 sections of the Mississippi state constitution. Whites were often coached on their

answers. Hamer failed the test, which asked about de facto laws.[1] "I knowed as much about a de facto law as a horse knows about Christmas Day," commented Hamer later.

On the way home, police stopped the old school bus in which Hamer and others who had tried to register were riding. The police fined the driver $100 because the bus was "too yellow" and could be mistaken for a real school bus. The bus had often carried plantation workers without any trouble until those same people wanted to vote.

---

1 **de facto laws:** laws that are in operation because of social or other customs but that may not be written and officially authorized

When she returned home, Fannie Lou Hamer was forced to leave the plantation, and her husband was eventually fired. Hamer began to work as a civil rights organizer. As she said: "There was nothing they could do to me. They couldn't fire me, because I didn't have a job. They couldn't put me out of my house, because I didn't have one. There was nothing they could take from me any longer."

In 1963, Fannie Lou Hamer successfully registered to vote on her third try. She helped organize the Mississippi Freedom Democratic party (MFDP), which held alternative elections to the all-white Mississippi Democratic party. At the 1964 Democratic National Convention in Atlantic City, New Jersey, the MFDP sought to be seated as the official Democratic delegation from Mississippi.

Fannie Lou Hamer testified on national television. "If the Freedom Democratic party is not seated now, I question America," she said. "Is this America, the land of the free and the home of the brave, where we have to sleep with our telephones off the hook because our lives be threatened daily, because we want to live as decent human beings in America?"

Hamer also described beatings she had received for attending voter registration meetings. President Lyndon Johnson scheduled a news conference to interrupt Hamer's televised testimony because he thought it might endanger his reelection.

Known for her powerful voice, Fannie Lou Hamer led the MFDP delegation in freedom songs on the convention floor. One reporter asked Hamer if she wanted equality with the white man. "No," she replied, "I don't want to go down that low. I want the true democracy that'll raise me and that white man up—raise America up."

The MFDP delegates were not seated in 1964. But Fannie Lou Hamer ran for Congress in an MFDP counter election to the regular Democratic primary. Although Hamer was not seated in Congress, the U.S. House of Representatives did investigate elections in Mississippi— and the federal courts eventually ruled them illegal. At the 1968 Democratic National Convention, Fannie Lou Hamer and her delegation from Mississippi were seated, to a standing ovation. From the cotton fields of Mississippi to the arenas of national politics, Fannie Lou Hamer was sick and tired no more.

Privacy and the Ninth Amendment

Justice Arthur Goldberg

In 1879, the state of Connecticut passed a law banning any drug or other product whose purpose was to prevent conception. In 1965, the case of Griswold v. Connecticut *came before the Supreme Court and challenged the constitutionality of that law. Estelle Griswold, executive director of the Planned Parenthood League of Connecticut, in violation of the law, gave out information and counseled married couples on preventing conception. She was arrested, convicted, and fined, and an appeals court upheld her conviction. However, in what became a landmark case on the issue of privacy, the Supreme Court overturned the previous decisions using the Ninth Amendment as the foundation. Following are excerpts from the statement of concurring justices Arthur Goldberg, William Brennan, and Chief Justice William O. Douglas, who wrote the majority opinion.*

The Court stated many years ago that the Due Process Clause protects those liberties that are "so rooted in the traditions and conscience of our people as to be ranked as fundamental.". . .

This Court, in a series of decisions, has held that the Fourteenth Amendment absorbs and applies to the States those specifics of the first eight amendments which express fundamental personal rights. The language and history of the Ninth Amendment reveal that the Framers of the Constitution believed that there are additional fundamental rights, protected from governmental infringement, which exist alongside those fundamental rights specifically mentioned in the first eight constitutional amendments. The Ninth Amendment reads, "The enumeration[1] in the Constitution, of certain rights, shall not be construed to deny or disparage[2] others retained by the people." The Amendment is almost entirely the work of James Madison. It was introduced in Congress by him, and passed

---

1 **enumeration:** naming one by one
2 **disparage:** regard as worthless

the House and Senate with little or no debate and virtually no change in language. It was proffered[3] to quiet expressed fears that a bill of specifically enumerated rights could not be sufficiently broad to cover all essential rights, and that the specific mention of certain rights would be interpreted as a denial that others were protected. . . .

While this Court has had little occasion to interpret the Ninth Amendment, "[i]t cannot be presumed that any clause in the Constitution is intended to be without effect" *[Marbury v. Madison, 1803]*.[4] In interpreting the Constitution, "real effect should be given to all the words it uses" *[Myers v. United States, 1926]*. The Ninth Amendment to the Constitution may be regarded by some as a recent discovery, and may be forgotten by others, but, since 1791, it has been a basic part of the Constitution which we are sworn to uphold. To hold that a right so basic and fundamental and so deep-rooted in our society as the right of privacy in marriage may be infringed because that right is not guaranteed in so many words by the first eight amendments to the Constitution is to ignore the Ninth Amendment, and to give it no effect whatsoever. . . .

In determining which rights are fundamental, judges are not left at large to decide cases in light of their personal and private notions. Rather, they must look to the "traditions and [collective] conscience of our people" to determine whether a principle is "so rooted [there] . . . as to be ranked as fundamental" *[Snyder v. Massachusetts, 1933]*. The inquiry is whether a right involved is of such a character that it cannot be denied without violating those "fundamental principles of liberty and justice which lie at the base of all our civil and political institutions" *[Snyder]*. . . .

I agree fully with the Court that . . . the right of privacy is a fundamental personal right, emanating[5] "from the totality of the constitutional scheme under which we live." Mr. Justice Brandeis, dissenting in *Olmstead v. United States, 1929*,[6] . . . summarized the principles underlying the Constitution's guarantees of privacy:

> The protection guaranteed by the [Fourth and Fifth]
> Amendments is much broader in scope. The makers of our
> Constitution undertook to secure conditions favorable to the

---

3 **proferred:** offered for acceptance

4 *Marbury v. Madison* was the first case to declare a law unconstitutional.

5 **emanating:** flowing outward

6 **Olmstead v. United States:** a Supreme Court case in which the judges decided that evidence obtained from a wiretap without a judge's order could be used without violating the Constitution

pursuit of happiness. They recognized the significance of man's spiritual nature of his feelings and of his intellect. They knew that only a part of the pain, pleasure and satisfactions of life are to be found in material things. They sought to protect Americans in their beliefs, their thoughts, their emotions and their sensations. They conferred, as against the Government, the right to be let alone—the most comprehensive of rights and the right most valued by civilized men.

The Connecticut statutes here involved deal with a particularly important and sensitive area of privacy—that of the marital relation and the marital home. . . . Certainly the safeguarding of the home does not follow merely from the sanctity of property rights. The home derives its preeminence as the seat of family life. And the integrity of that life is something so fundamental that it has been found to draw to its protection the principles of more than one explicitly granted Constitutional right. . . . Of this whole "private realm of family life," it is difficult to imagine what is more private or more intimate than a husband and wife's marital relations.

The entire fabric of the Constitution and the purposes that clearly underlie its specific guarantees demonstrate that the rights to marital privacy and to marry and raise a family are of similar order and magnitude as the fundamental rights specifically protected. Although the Constitution does not speak in so many words of the right of privacy in marriage, I cannot believe that it offers these fundamental rights no protection. The fact that no particular provision of the Constitution explicitly forbids the State from disrupting the traditional relation of the family—a relation as old and as fundamental as our entire civilization—surely does not show that the Government was meant to have the power to do so. Rather, as the Ninth Amendment expressly recognizes, there are fundamental personal rights such as this one, which are protected from abridgment by the Government, though not specifically mentioned in the Constitution. . . .

. . . In sum, I believe that the right of privacy in the marital relation is fundamental and basic—a personal right "retained by the people" within the meaning of the Ninth Amendment. Connecticut cannot constitutionally abridge this fundamental right, which is protected by the Fourteenth Amendment from infringement by the States. I agree with the Court that petitioners' convictions must therefore be reversed.

The Rights of Americans with Disabilities

The Atlanta Legal Aid Society (ALAS) in Georgia provides legal services for poor people. In 1995, the ALAS took on the case of Lois Curtis and Elaine Wilson, known publicly only by their initials L.C. and E.W., who had been diagnosed with mental retardation, schizophrenia, and/or personality disorder and confined to institutions. Mental health evaluators determined they were better suited for living in the community, and the women wanted the greater freedom, but the state of Georgia argued for the right to keep persons with disabilities in institutionalized settings. The case, Olmstead v. L.C. and E.W., made its way to the Supreme Court in 1999 and a 6–3 court delivered a landmark ruling in favor of L.C. and E.W. The selections that follow are from the archives of the Atlanta Legal Aid Society.

Background

Olmstead v. L.C. and E.W.

[When this case was first brought to court] in the Eleventh Circuit[, it] sought community residential placements for L.C. and E.W. who had spent the majority of their lives in mental institutions. For several years, their treatment teams acknowledged that they no longer met the requirements for involuntary confinement, but refused to release them to a community-based program with appropriate services. The case, filed in 1995, presents a claim under the Americans with Disabilities Act (ADA). Our position is that the State of Georgia can no longer provide disability services to a mentally or physically disabled person in an institutional setting if he or she could be served in a more integrated, community-based setting. The State appealed a favorable decision of the federal District Court granting summary judgment[1] for our plaintiffs.[2] Oral argument before the Eleventh Circuit Court of Appeals was in November 1997. The Eleventh Circuit ruled that the State's failure to provide integrated community services under these circumstances violated the Americans with Disabilities Act.

The State appealed to the United States Supreme Court to reverse that ruling. Now known as *Olmstead v. L.C. and E.W.*, it was heard on April 21, 1999. This [was] the first U.S. Supreme Court case involving the "integration mandate" of the Americans with Disabilities Act. Although both plaintiffs were [finally] receiving community services in response to the lawsuit, the case continued because the State of Georgia had not changed its policies, and the situation could have arisen again.

After L.C. and E.W. moved from institutional life into the community, each progressed in ways that reveal the monotony[3] of their former circumstances—for example, L.C. likes long neighborhood walks and has (after many years) reconnected with her mom and sister. She visits the mall and picks out her own clothes. She has favorite meals and has learned to plan a menu. She quit a 3-pack a day cigarette habit. She speaks clearly and communicates well. She has two close friends at the group home. She loved her first airplane trip to Washington, and her meeting with a variety of media in connection with the Supreme Court consideration of her case.

E.W. spent a year in a group home, where she decorated her own room, organized picture albums, and made regular weekend trips home to be with her extended family. She lived in a house with a caretaker and friend, who worked during the day while E.W. was at her pre-vocational program.[4] E.W. became increasingly independent, taking complete responsibility for her own medical needs, an area that institutional doctors felt was problematic; [she] was able to shop, cook, choose her own clothes, and attend family events and celebrations.

---

1 **summary judgment:** court decision without a trial when there is no dispute about the facts
2 **plaintiffs:** the people who initiate a court case
3 **monotony:** lack of variety; repetitiveness
4 **pre-vocational program:** instruction to prepare for vocational school

Reactions to the Day in the Supreme Court, April 21, 1999

Several Legal Aid lawyers, the Board's President, and the Vice President attended the argument. Most used words such as "awe-inspiring" and "re-energizing" to describe the experience.

Sue Jamieson, [lead counsel for Legal Aid's clients]:

The two legal aid clients who were Plaintiffs in this case were, like each of our clients, people with little income and, by conventional standards, undervalued. We represented them simply because they called our office— exactly why we represent all of our clients. The fact that we filed a case in federal court raising an ADA claim is mostly because unnecessary institutionalization of people is the most egregious[5] of the many wrongs endured by our clients with mental disabilities— like spousal abuse, illegal evictions, consumer fraud, etc., etc., etc. . . . The case began like all our cases with the everyday effort to represent someone who called the office.

The question these clients asked was, in essence, "Can you help me out of this outrageous situation?"—the question we are asked every day over and over and over.

How the question ended up in the Supreme Court is as random as the lottery. Fewer than 100 of 7,000 petitions for certiorari[6] are granted each year. . . . Somehow, one of those many questions got blown up to an exaggerated size, just one of our many questions that we all

(left to right) Sue Jameison, Elaine Wilson, Lois Curtis

persist in asking daily in our work, hoping to shift the balance slightly.

What a great feeling it was to be annoying the Supreme Court with one of our clients' questions! . . .

Judge Patsy Y. Porter, 1999 ALAS President:

I was both proud and humbled to be there. We have an awesome responsibility. The things we do affect everyone's lives. Win, lose or draw, I still think we win because we stand up for the rights of people who would not otherwise have a voice. That in itself is why we have Legal Aid. We are protecting the Constitutional rights of everyone in this country. And no matter what happens now, we have done the right thing for these clients.

---

5 **egregious:** seriously bad or shocking
6 **certiorari:** requests that a higher court review a decision or case of a lower court ruling

Final Result

On July 11, 2000, in the courtroom of Judge Marvin Shoob, the *L.C. and E.W. v. Olmstead* case came to a formal close with the signing of the final settlement agreement.

Sue Jamieson, lead counsel for Legal Aid's clients, began with a presentation crediting the lawyers that were involved, the courage of the clients, and the judicial pioneering of Judge Shoob for this milestone. Sue described the long litigation[7] road, and the benefits of the settlement to the clients.

The court then called on the *guardian ad litem*,[8] Jonathan Zimring, who had high praise for the legal team that represented his clients.

Perhaps the most moving statements came from the clients themselves, who were invited to address the court. Lois said that now that the case was over, she hoped it would help other people. Elaine said that now she feels loved and cared for where she lives. In the institution, she had felt like she was sitting in a little box with no way out. They both spoke of little things, such as making Kool Aid and being outdoors, that meant so much to them.

Judge Shoob then called on Steve Gottlieb, Executive Director of Atlanta Legal Aid, who mentioned that the case had been portrayed as the *Brown v. Board of Education* of disability law, and as a defining moment in the Americans with Disabilities Act.

Judge Shoob then declared that the settlement agreement was approved and was now in effect. He complimented Sue Jamieson, [Attorney] David Webster, and others for what he described as an outstanding effort and a splendid result.

---

7 **litigation:** legal proceeding

8 ***guardian ad litem:*** a legal guardian of a person or persons appointed by the state to advocate for those under their guardianship

The Death of a Hero—Ms. Elaine Wilson, 53, died on December 5, 2004. She was a plaintiff in the case *L.C. and E.W. v. Olmstead,* decided by the United States Supreme Court in 1999. The case was filed against the state of Georgia, alleging that the Plaintiffs were being segregated in a psychiatric institution when, with proper supports, they could live a more normal, community-based life. Ms. Wilson intervened in the case in 1995, claiming along with her co-plaintiff, Lois Curtis, that she was being segregated unnecessarily in a state hospital in Georgia. . . .

After filing the case, Ms. Wilson was provided with community services and she lived in a home with a friend and care provider. Although she had been institutionalized more than 30 times prior to bringing the lawsuit, once she was provided with alternative community-based options, she enjoyed an active life in the community. She developed her own advocacy skills, speaking and presenting in Georgia and in other places in the country about her own experiences and her hopes for the freedom of other institutionalized persons. She was known and loved by many in the disability community who were inspired by her determination and interest in reaching out to others once she finally secured her own freedom.

In states such as New York, where the above vigil took place, laws in the early 1990s called for closing state mental institutions and using the savings to provide community care for the mentally ill. However, in many places, the savings were never passed along, and many mentally ill people ended up homeless.

Pastel drawing by Lois Curtis. Photographed by Robin Nelson.

Lois Curtis: Folk Artist—Lois Curtis, one of the original *Olmstead* plaintiffs, has been busy since being freed from a lifetime of repeated institutionalizations. She enjoys living on her own, with the aid of community-based services; she has reconnected with her family, and she has made new friends.

Her own experiences with institutionalization, and the Supreme Court case that freed her, have prompted a passion for advocacy. "I want to tell everybody, so people can get out." The Tubman African American Museum recognized Lois with the 'Act of Courage Award' for "standing up and taking action during challenging circumstances to make a difference for yourself and the lives of others."

Lois has also found success as a folk artist, and has had several well-received shows at several galleries, including Arts for All Gallery in the Healy Building in downtown Atlanta, the Temple Gallery in Decatur, and other galleries throughout the U.S.

You Get Proud
by Practicing

Laura Hershey

The Civil Rights movement made great strides for African Americans and women during the 1960s, but it was not until the 1990s that Americans with disabilities won similar legislation, notably the Americans with Disabilities Act of 1990. Laura Hershey was one of many who fought for equal rights and for accommodations that would greatly increase the independence of Americans with disabilities.

If you are not proud
For who you are, for what you say, for how you look;
If every time you stop
To think of yourself, you do not see yourself glowing
With golden light; do not, therefore, give up on yourself.
You can get proud.

You do not need
A better body, a purer spirit, or a Ph.D.
To be proud.
You do not need
A lot of money, a handsome boyfriend, or a nice car.
You do not need
To be able to walk, or see, or hear,
Or use big, complicated words,
Or do any of the things that you just can't do
To be proud. A caseworker
Cannot make you proud,
Or a doctor.

You only need more practice.
You get proud by practicing.

There are many many ways to get proud.
You can try riding a horse, or skiing on one leg,
Or playing guitar,
And do well or not so well,
And be glad you tried
Either way.
You can show
Something you've made
To someone you respect
And be happy with it no matter
What they say.
You can say
What you think, though you know
Other people do not think the same way, and you can
Keep saying it, even if they tell you
You are crazy.

You can add your voice
All night to the voices
Of a hundred and fifty others
In a circle
Around a jailhouse
Where your brothers and sisters are being held
For blocking buses with no lifts,
Or you can be one of the ones
Inside the jailhouse,
Knowing of the circle outside.
You can speak your love
To a friend
Without fear.
You can find someone who will listen to you
Without judging you or doubting you or being
Afraid of you
And let you hear yourself perhaps
For the first time.
These are all ways
Of getting proud.
None of them

Are easy, but all of them
Are possible. You can do all of these things,
Or just one of them again and again.
You get proud
By practicing.

Power makes you proud, and power
Comes in many fine forms
Supple and rich as butterfly wings.
It is music
When you practice opening your mouth
And liking what you hear
Because it is the sound of your own
True voice.
It is sunlight
When you practice seeing
Strength and beauty in everyone
Including yourself.
It is dance when you practice knowing
That what you do
And the way you do it
Is the right way for you
And cannot be called wrong.
All these hold
More power than weapons or money
Or lies.
All these practices bring power, and power
Makes you proud.
You get proud
By practicing.

Remember, you weren't the one
Who made you ashamed,
But you are the one
Who can make you proud.
Just practice,
Practice until you get proud, and once you are proud,
Keep practicing so you won't forget.
You get proud
By practicing.

Putting the Second Amendment Second

Akhil Reed Amar

When people disagree on the meaning of the Second Amendment, they often divide into two camps. Those who support strong gun control measures read the amendment to say that the federal government cannot prevent states from arming their own militias, but the right to arm does not extend to individuals. In contrast, those who support gun rights read the amendment to say that individuals, not just collective militias, have the right to own firearms. In broader legal terms, the question the courts have grappled with as they have considered Second Amendment cases is this: Does the Second Amendment apply to the states or just to the national government? In other words, can states ban handguns and other firearms or does the Constitution require that states allow gun ownership? Two recent cases have begun to clarify the Supreme Court's position on this question. One, District of Columbia v. Heller *(2008), challenged the longstanding ban on handguns in the District of Columbia with the case of an armed security guard who was not allowed to bring a gun into his home for self-protection. The other,* McDonald v. Chicago *(2010), similarly challenged Chicago's handgun ban. Law professor Akhil Reed Amar considers the constitutional issues in these cases.*

The language of the Second Amendment has been the obsessive focus of just about everyone interested in *District of Columbia v. Heller,* the D.C. gun-ownership case. . . That amendment is indeed important and much misunderstood. But Heller's facts, which involve the possession of a gun inside the home for self-defense, lie rather far from the Second Amendment's core concerns, as originally understood by the Founding Fathers. To think straight about gun control and the Constitution, we need to move past the Second Amendment and pay more heed to the Ninth and 14th Amendments.

Let's begin here: Suppose, for argument's sake, that we concede that everything gun-control advocates say about the Second Amendment is right. Suppose that the amendment focused solely on arms-bearing in military contexts, and that it said absolutely nothing about an individual's right to have a gun while sleeping in his own home or hunting in his own private Idaho. Would this concession mean that no individual constitutional right exists today?

Hardly. According to the Ninth Amendment: "The enumeration[1] in the Constitution of certain rights shall not be construed to deny or disparage other rights retained by the people." In other words, there may well be constitutional rights that are not explicitly set forth in the Second Amendment (or in any other amendment or constitutional clause, for that matter). In identifying these unenumerated "rights retained by the people," the key is that a judge should not decide what he or she personally thinks would be a proper set of rights. Instead, the judge should ask which rights have been recognized by the American people themselves—for example, in state constitutions and state bills of rights and civil rights laws. Americans have also established, merely by living

---

1 **enumeration:** naming one by one

our lives freely across the country and over the centuries, certain customary rights that governments have generally respected. Many of our most basic rights are simply facts of life, the residue of a virtually unchallenged pattern and practice on the ground in domains where citizens act freely and governments lie low.

Consider, for example, the famous 1965 privacy case *Griswold v. Connecticut.*[2] The state of Connecticut purported[3] to criminalize the use of contraception, even by married couples, prompting the Supreme Court to strike down this extraordinarily intrusive[4] state law as unconstitutional. Writing for the majority, Justice William Douglas claimed that a general right of privacy could be found in between the lines of the Bill of Rights. But Douglas did a poor job of proving his case. . . . Writing separately in *Griswold,* the second Justice John Harlan, widely admired for his judicial care and craftsmanship, offered a more modest and less strained rationale: "Conclusive, in my view, is the utter novelty of [Connecticut's] enactment. Although the Federal Government and many States have at one time or another had on their books statutes forbidding the distribution of contraceptives, none, so far as I can find, has made the use of contraceptives a crime." Thus, the basic practice of the American people rendered Connecticut's oddball law presumptively[5] unconstitutional. It is also highly noteworthy that today around a dozen state constitutions and countless statutes speak explicitly of a right to privacy—a right nowhere explicitly mentioned in the federal Constitution.

Now take Harlan's sensible approach to the unenumerated right of privacy and apply it to Dick Anthony Heller's claim that he has a right to have a gun in his D.C. home for self-defense. When we look at the actual pattern of lived rights in America—what the people have, in fact, done—we find lots of regulations of guns, but few outright prohibitions of guns in homes as sweeping as the D.C. ordinance. We also find a right to keep guns affirmed in a great many modern state constitutions, several of which use the phrase "bear arms" in ways that clearly go beyond the military context. Unlike founding-era documents, modern state constitutions routinely affirm a constitutional right to "bear arms" for hunting, recreation, and/or self-defense.

---

2 See pages 62–65 for more on *Griswold* v. *Connecticut.*
3 **purported:** claimed
4 **intrustive:** unwelcome and disruptive
5 **presumptively:** on the basis of a reasonable assumption

In addition to the Ninth Amendment, we should also view the right to bear arms through the lens of the 14th Amendment's command that "No state shall make or enforce any law which shall abridge the privileges or immunities of citizens of the United States." Though this particular sentence applies only to the states, other language in the 14th Amendment affirms that the federal government, too, has a parallel obligation to respect the fundamental rights of citizens.

But the 14th Amendment did not specifically enumerate these sacred privileges and immunities. Instead, like the Ninth, the 14th invited interpreters to pay close attention to fundamental rights that Americans had affirmed through their lived experience—in state bills of rights and in other canonical[6] texts such as the Declaration of Independence and landmark civil rights legislation. And when it came to guns, a companion statute to the 14th Amendment, enacted by Congress in 1866, declared that "laws . . . concerning personal liberty [and] personal security . . . including the constitutional right to bear arms, shall be secured to and enjoyed by all the citizens." Here, in sharp contrast to founding-era legal texts, the "bear arms" phrase was decisively severed[7] from the military context. Women as well as men could claim a "personal" right to protect their "personal liberty" and "personal security" in their homes. The Reconstruction-era Congress clearly understood that Southern blacks might need guns in their homes to protect themselves from private violence in places where they could not rely on local constables to keep their neighborhoods safe. When guns were outlawed, only outlaw Klansmen would have guns, to paraphrase a modern NRA slogan.[8] In this critical chapter in the history of American liberty, we find additional evidence of an individual right to have a gun in one's home, regardless of the original meaning of the Second Amendment.

There are at least three advantages in shifting 21st-century gun-control discourse in this direction. First, a Ninth-and-14th Amendment framework is more modest. Unusually draconian[9] gun laws can be struck down simply because they lie outside the lived pattern of the American experience, while more mainstream gun laws can be upheld precisely because they have proved acceptable to the people in many places. If our

---

6 **canonical:** accepted as authoritative and essential

7 **severed:** broken off

8 **NRA slogan:** "If you outlaw guns, only outlaws will have guns."

9 **draconian:** harsh and unforgiving, named after Draco, who established a harsh legal code in ancient Athens

nation's capital wants to argue that specially strict gun rules should apply there because the city faces unique risks, no rigid textual language prevents judges from considering such pragmatic[10] claims in the course of interpreting the boundaries of actual American practice. By contrast, if the Second Amendment's language really did guarantee a right to guns in homes, by what authority could judges allow for a different approach in D.C.? And then, if one has a Second Amendment right to a pistol or shotgun at home, why not a machine gun? Given that the Second Amendment's core right is military, it would seem odd that military arms would be easier to ban than other weapons.

Second, the Ninth and 14th Amendments are more modern and democratically responsive. The Ninth invites us to consider not only rights that have long been part of the American tradition but also rights that have emerged in actual modern practice and in state constitutional clauses of relatively recent vintage that are relatively easy to amend. The 14th directs our attention to the still-relevant problems of race and police protection or the absence thereof. By contrast, the Second Amendment harkens back to a lost 18th-century America, where citizens regularly mustered[11] for militia service on the town square and where the federal army was rightly suspect. This is not our world.

Finally, a focus on the Ninth and 14th Amendments is simply more honest. The open-ended language of the Ninth and 14th Amendments really did aim to invite Americans to ponder state constitutional provisions that declare rights, and these provisions really do focus on individual self-defense. The framers of the 14th Amendment really did focus intently on self-defense in the home. The framers of the Second did not.

---

10 **pragmatic:** practical
11 **mustered:** assembled

RESPONDING TO CLUSTER TWO

HOW WELL DOES FEDERALISM PROTECT INDIVIDUAL RIGHTS?

Critical Thinking Skill   DEFINING KEY WORDS AND PHRASES

1. In his "Spirit of Liberty" speech, Judge Learned Hand asks what liberty is, but he does not directly answer that question. Instead, he explains what it is *not,* and then continues describing what the spirit of liberty *does.* According to Hand, what is liberty *not?* What does the spirit of liberty *do?* Using these ideas, try to define what liberty *is.*

2. Explain the reasoning behind the *Brown v. Board of Education* decision that by definition "separate" cannot be "equal." Refer to "The Doll Test and the Fourteenth Amendment" selection to formulate your answer.

3. Compare the language in the book excerpt "The Courage of Their Convictions: Fannie Lou Hamer" with that in the excerpts from the Supreme Court opinion in the Griswold case ("Privacy and the Ninth Amendment"). Identify three ways in which the language differs and explain the effect of the language in each selection on its impact. You can use a chart like the one below to organize your comparison.

Language in Fannie Lou Hamer	Language in Supreme Court Opinion
1.	1.
2.	2.
3.	3.
Impact:	Impact:

4. What do the words that form the title and refrain of Laura Hershey's poem "You Get Proud by Practicing" mean? Explain your answer using the examples of Lois Curtis and Elaine Wilson, the persons with disabilities highlighted in the selection "The Rights of Americans with Disabilities."

5. What two meanings have people read into the phrase "the right to bear arms"? Does Reed's argument in "Putting the Second Amendment Second" favor one of these? If so, which one?

Writing Activity: Extend a Definition

Analyze the selections in this cluster, considering what the term *liberty* means in the context of each of the readings. Write an essay in which you explain the various meanings and draw conclusions about the federal government's role in protecting liberty.

A Strong Extended Definition

* considers multiple meanings in different contexts
* often helps clarify definitions by showing what something is not
* often shows the concept in action

CLUSTER THREE

WHY ARE SUSPECTS' RIGHTS IMPORTANT?

Critical Thinking Skill
INTEGRATING MULTIMEDIA INFORMATION

Atoms vs. Bits: Your Phone in the Eyes of the Law

Alexis Madrigal

Changing technology has created new issues in privacy. For example, it is well established that police need a warrant to search your home. What about your cell phone, though, which can often contain as much sensitive information as the inside of a home? In the article that follows, Alexis Madrigal analyzes the legal issues related to the new technology.

On the last Friday in November in 2007, James Nix was riding shotgun in a car driving through the streets of Albany, Oregon, a freeway passthrough town between Salem and Eugene. Nix had several outstanding warrants for possession of a controlled substance, endangering the welfare of a minor and violating his parole on an earlier drug conviction. Earlier that day, an Albany police officer saw Nix take a call on his cell and then immediately after sell drugs to someone in [a] classic hand-to-hand, money for drugs, switch. So, he'd tipped off another officer by the name of Jones to watch for the car. After investigating Nix for several weeks, they were going to make an arrest.

Officer Jones pulled Nix's friend over in a lawful traffic stop and Nix bolted. He didn't get far before being apprehended, though, and Jones patted him down, finding 22 clear plastic baggies often associated with drug dealing, $370 in cash and a cellphone. Jones said while he counted the money, the phone rang "continually." With enough evidence to make an arrest for selling drugs, Jones called Nix's investigators, who told him to deliver the phone to the Albany [Police Department']s mobile phone expert. Without a warrant, the forensics[1] analyst searched the entire contents of the phone and "found text messages that he believed were

---

1 **forensics:** the application of scientific methodology to criminal cases

drug related and images 'consistent with methamphetamine.'"[2] They were subsequently used against Nix in a trial which found him guilty.

Ask yourself: Do you think it was OK for the police to search the contents of Nix's phone without a warrant?

It's a complicated issue. We have rules against warrantless searches for good reason. On the other hand, law enforcement doesn't want to lose the ability to do everything it can to catch people they think are criminals.

Here's the legal issue at the heart of the case, which was argued before the Oregon Supreme Court [in May 2011]. We all know that the Fourth Amendment to the Constitution protects everyone from "unreasonable" search and seizure. Since the 18th century, though, many cases have touched on how to define what is and is not unreasonable. Under English common law, it was generally considered reasonable for the police to search you while you were being arrested. It became known as the "search incident to arrest exception" and has been around in American law for well over 100 years. The big change to the exception came in the 1969 case *Chimel vs. California,* which laid out a key exception to the exception. Namely, if a suspect was arrested in his home, the police couldn't search his whole house. As Wikipedia summarizes it, the police could only search, "the area within the immediate control of the suspect," or as James Nix's attorney Bronson James more colorfully put it, there is a "wingspan rule." If you can reach it, the cops can search it.

Since then, there have been a variety of exceptions to the exceptions to the exceptions as courts try to grapple[3] with the definition of "unreasonable." Courts have said that some types of objects near you are searchable—purses, backpacks, diaries, etc.—but that others might not be, like, say, a trunk.

Cellphones, indeed all digital devices, complicate the whole idea. Defense attorney James argued in a brief he filed this month that cellphones, as receptacles of bits, needed protections that objects made of atoms simply did not.

Framing the search incident to arrest doctrine in terms of purses and backpacks no longer works. . . . Such a container is constrained by its

---

2 **methamphetamine:** a highly addictive and restricted or illegal drug
3 **grapple:** struggle; wrestle

physicality.[4] It can hold only so much. It is finite. And as such, the privacy intrusion in searching a physical container is also finite.

But [cellphones and other devices] are not containers so much as portals.[5] They themselves hold a vast amount of information, but also hold access to cloud information. They can hold anything, and are infinite. And, correspondingly, the privacy invasion of a full search of their contents is potentially infinite.

But the Oregon Appellate Court didn't agree. They argued that there really wasn't anything so novel[6] about "cellular telephones" and that old analogies worked just fine.

"The premise[7] of defendant's arguments is that cellular telephones are so special, indeed unique, in their character and capacity that they must be treated differently than other receptacles of possible evidence of crimes—including, for example, 'day-timers,' calendars, address books, letters and even diaries—in a defendant's possession at the time of arrest," the court wrote. "Ultimately, on a fully developed record, there could be some merit to that claim. But, even in this Wi-Fi age, it is hardly a self-evident—much less judicially noticeable—proposition, factually or legally."

I'm not a legal scholar, but it does seem self-evident to me that a cellphone like mine containing 14,000 text messages, all of my Facebook and phone contacts, hundreds of photographs, access through Gmail to my entire e-mail history, location data going back more than a year and every Web site I've ever visited on it is qualitatively different from an address book. And the smarter our phones get, the more different they become. As everyone in the technology world has said out loud or to themselves at one point or another, we're all carrying computers in our pockets, computers that hold location data tied to everything we do and connect through the Internet to many, many facets of our lives. Should it take a warrant to access that universe? Boy, I hope so, but some of the case law seems to make *physical size* the key attribute on which the need for a warrant turns. In an era of miniaturization of computer memory, that's just ludicrous.[8]

---

4 **physicality:** predominantly physical or material, sometimes at the expense of the spiritual, emotional, or social

5 **portals:** doorways

6 **novel:** new, unusual, interesting

7 **premise:** a statement helping to support a conclusion in logic-based arguments

8 **ludicrous:** laughably foolish

Nix's attorney, James, argues that we should think of phones as something more akin to our homes. If there is going to be a historical analogy made, he thinks we've got to go all the way back to the reasons that the Fourth Amendment came into being.

"The Fourth Amendment talks a lot about the protection of the home because the things that you valued most in your life were most likely to be found in your home: your letters, your records, your possessions, your strongbox full of money. They were all tangible objects that resided in your house," James told me. "Now, there is no strongbox of money, but my iPhone does have a permanent connection to Wells Fargo. My medicine and health records are not sitting in my home but I do have a Providence Health app. My e-mail is my correspondence. As the technology has progressed, it has enabled us to shrink the home and carry it around in our pocket. The capability of our technology to miniaturize cannot therefore also minimize constitutional protections."

How Teens (12-17) Use Cell Phones Beyond Texting and Making Calls

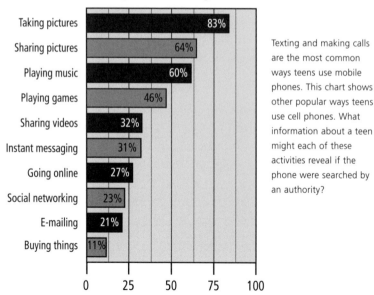

Taking pictures — 83%
Sharing pictures — 64%
Playing music — 60%
Playing games — 46%
Sharing videos — 32%
Instant messaging — 31%
Going online — 27%
Social networking — 23%
E-mailing — 21%
Buying things — 11%

Texting and making calls are the most common ways teens use mobile phones. This chart shows other popular ways teens use cell phones. What information about a teen might each of these activities reveal if the phone were searched by an authority?

Nationally, both the Ohio and California supreme courts have taken on the question of warrantless cellphone searches. The Ohio Supreme Court ruled that the searches did violate the Fourth Amendment, although three judges dissented saying searching cell phones was analogous to searching address books. (I make the obvious observation that perhaps those justices' cellphones are quite like an address book, but mine certainly is not.) California, on the other hand, held that the phone was "immediately associated" with the defendant and therefore searchable.

The Electronic Frontier Foundation[9] has been active in these battles, too. The EFF filed a brief of amicus curiae[10] in support of James's case. They note that "the touchstone question" for any Fourth Amendment case is whether an individual "has a reasonable expectation of privacy." Of course, because everyone has personal information stored on cellphones many courts have found that people have a reasonable expectation of privacy with regard to the phone's data.

If warrantless cellphone searches are allowed, any time someone is arrested carrying a phone—so almost always—the government will be able to comb through everything that they are able to access through the phone and with the help of the best tools that mobile forensics can provide.

"If the court accepts the government's position, a person's digital life will be an open book for law enforcement whenever the owner of a device is arrested," the EFF concluded. . . .

What's really at issue here is whether it's the size of the digital device that matters or the amount of information it contains. It's a classic case where if you think about it in terms of the atoms—the stuff —you get one answer but if you think about it in terms of bits you get another. The phone is small, so it is easy to have it "immediately associated" with you. But the information it contains is vast and wide-reaching and valuable.

The battle points out just how tuned our laws are to our bodies. Remember the wingspan rule or the plain view doctrine, which presupposes[11] a certain resolution for your eyes? These things only make sense in the world of atoms. And we don't yet have new rules for that other, constantly growing world of bits.

---

9 **Electronic Frontier Foundation:** an organization devoted to "defending free speech, privacy, innovation, and consumer rights"

10 **amicus curiae:** a Latin term meaning "friend of the court." This refers to someone who is not a party to the case but who is an advisor to the court on some aspect of the case.

11 **presupposes:** takes for granted

Nineteen Eighty-Four

George Orwell

Orwell's famous novel, written in 1949, paints a bleak picture of a society in which war and government surveillance are constant.

It was a bright cold day in April, and the clocks were striking thirteen. Winston Smith, his chin nuzzled into his breast in an effort to escape the vile wind, slipped quickly through the glass doors of Victory Mansions, though not quickly enough to prevent a swirl of gritty dust from entering along with him.

The hallway smelt of boiled cabbage and old rag mats. At one end of it a coloured poster, too large for indoor display, had been tacked to the wall. It depicted simply an enormous face, more than a metre wide: the face of a man of about forty-five, with a heavy black moustache and ruggedly handsome features. Winston made for the stairs. It was no use trying the lift.[1] Even at the best of times it was seldom working, and at present the electric current was cut off during daylight hours. It was part of the economy drive in preparation for Hate Week. The flat[2] was seven flights up, and Winston, who was thirty-nine and had a varicose ulcer[3] above his right ankle, went slowly, resting several times on the way. On each landing, opposite the lift-shaft, the poster with the enormous face gazed from the wall. It was one of those pictures which are so contrived[4] that the eyes follow you about when you move. BIG BROTHER IS WATCHING YOU, the caption beneath it ran.

Inside the flat a fruity voice was reading out a list of figures which had something to do with the production of pig-iron. The voice came from an oblong metal plaque like a dulled mirror which formed part of the surface of the right-hand wall. Winston turned a switch and the voice

---

1 **lift:** elevator
2 **flat:** apartment
3 **varicose ulcer:** a chronic wound
4 **contrived:** deliberately created

sank somewhat, though the words were still distinguishable. The instrument (the telescreen, it was called) could be dimmed, but there was no way of shutting it off completely. He moved over to the window: a smallish, frail figure, the meagreness of his body merely emphasized by the blue overalls which were the uniform of the party. His hair was very fair, his face naturally sanguine,[5] his skin roughened by coarse soap and blunt razor blades and the cold of the winter that had just ended.

Outside, even through the shut window-pane, the world looked cold. Down in the street little eddies of wind were whirling dust and torn paper into spirals, and though the sun was shining and the sky a harsh blue, there seemed to be no colour in anything, except the posters that were plastered everywhere. The black moustachio'd face gazed down from every commanding corner. There was one on the house-front immediately opposite. BIG BROTHER IS WATCHING YOU, the caption said, while the dark eyes looked deep into Winston's own. Down at street level another poster, torn at one corner, flapped fitfully in the wind, alternately covering and uncovering the single word INGSOC.[6] In the far distance a helicopter skimmed down between the roofs, hovered for an instant like a bluebottle,[7] and darted away again with a curving flight. It was the police patrol, snooping into people's windows. The patrols did not matter, however. Only the Thought Police mattered.

Behind Winston's back the voice from the telescreen was still babbling away about pig-iron and the overfulfilment of the Ninth Three-Year Plan. The telescreen received and transmitted simultaneously. Any sound that Winston made, above the level of a very low whisper, would be picked up by it, moreover, so long as he remained within the field of vision which the metal plaque commanded, he could be seen as well as heard. There was of course no way of knowing whether you were being watched at any given moment. How often, or on what system, the Thought Police plugged in on any individual wire was guesswork. It was even conceivable that they watched everybody all the time. But at any rate they could plug in your wire whenever they wanted to. You had to live—did live, from habit that became instinct—in the assumption that every sound you made was overheard, and, except in darkness, every movement scrutinized.

---

5 **sanguine:** ruddy; blood-red
6 **INGSOC:** Ingsoc stands for "English Socialism," the fictitious political system in the world of the novel.
7 **bluebottle:** type of fly

THE WORK OF BROTHERS

DALE WISELY

On Tuesday, September 11, 2001, nineteen terrorists tied to the militant Islamic group al-Qaeda hijacked four airplanes intended for suicide attacks on the United States. Two planes hit the World Trade Center in New York, and a third hit the Pentagon in Washington, D.C. On the fourth flight, passengers overtook the hijackers to prevent them from hitting another target, and the plane crashed on a Pennsylvania field, killing all aboard. Within weeks, the government set up the new Department of Homeland Security which, in its effort to protect the United States from attack, has raised questions about individual rights. Within only minutes, however, New York firefighters were already at work trying to rescue as many people as possible. The first plane hit the north tower of the World Trade Center at 8:46 a.m.; by 8:50 firefighters had set up a command post at "ground zero." Hundreds gave their lives to save others.

Firemen
find a brother in the rubble.
After so many days,
the body should be hard to take.
And yet, as they wrap him in the flag,
they speak to the corpse.

Don't worry about it.
Don't you worry about it, Mike.
You're all right. You're all right.
We're carrying you out of here.

And from the hands of one
to the hands of another
and then to another
down the line,
across smoldering hills
and valleys never meant to be,
they pass their brother
home.

New York City firefighters raise the flag at Ground Zero—the World Trade
Center—the afternoon of September 11, 2001.

The Civil Rights of American Muslims After 9/11

Abdus Sattar Ghazali

The nation's founders believed so strongly in protecting the rights of suspects that they enshrined those rights in the 4th, 5th, 6th, and 8th amendments of the Constitution. (See pages 10–11.) These amendments guarantee protection from unreasonable searches and seizures, the right to due process of law, the right to a speedy public trial by jury in which the accusers must face the accused with specific charges, the right to an attorney, and protection against cruel and unusual punishment. When the nation is in a crisis, however, is it appropriate to limit some of those liberties to protect national security? In the following excerpts from a report, a journalist provides one perspective on how the 9/11 terrorist attacks and the national security policies that grew out of them affected the civil rights of American Muslims.

On September 11, 2001, Muslim leaders gathered in Washington for a meeting with President George Bush to discuss, among other issues facing the Muslim community, the fulfillment of his election pledge to abrogate[1] the Secret Evidence Act of 1995 that was mainly used against Muslims. The Bush pledge had come during his election campaign meeting with the Muslim leaders. He had also challenged the use of secret evidence at the second presidential debate. His pledge led to en bloc[2] Muslim vote for Bush in 2000.

However, this all changed on 9/11. The meeting was aborted while more stringent[3] laws were introduced in the aftermath of the terrorist

---

1 **abrogate:** abolish
2 **en bloc:** as a single unit
3 **stringent:** strict

attacks on New York and Washington that significantly curtailed the civil rights of Muslims. . . .[4]

The sweeping antiterrorism legislation known as the USA PATRIOT Act was rushed through Congress and signed into law by President Bush on October 26, 2001. The USA PATRIOT Act is the acronym for "Uniting and Strengthening America by Providing Appropriate Tools Required to Intercept and Obstruct Terrorism Act." The law was passed without meaningful review by a panicked Congress just six weeks after the 9/11 terrorist attacks. The legislation flew through the House 357 to 66 and the Senate 99 to 1 . . . on Oct. 25, 2001 and [was] signed into law by President Bush the next day. With the rubble of the World Trade Center and the Pentagon still smoking, obviously it was difficult to resist. . . .

With this law sweeping new powers were given to both domestic law enforcement and international intelligence agencies, and [it] eliminated the checks and balances that [had been] put into place after previous misuse of surveillance powers by these agencies, including the revelation in 1974 that the FBI and foreign intelligence agencies had spied on over 10,000 U.S. citizens, including Martin Luther King Jr. The USA PATRIOT Act gave the government broad new powers to detain non-citizens indefinitely and to conduct searches, seizures, and surveillance with reduced standards of cause and levels of judicial review, among other provisions. Prior to September 11, 2001, many of these provisions would [have been] considered an unthinkable and unconstitutional violation of cherished U.S. ideals of privacy from unwarranted governmental intrusion and of individual rights.

On March 9, 2006, President Bush signed a new version of the USA PATRIOT Act that permanently extends 14 of 16 expiring provisions of the PATRIOT Act. Congressman Pete Stark, who voted against the reauthorization of the Act, sums up the controversial provisions of the Act:

> The government can still listen in on your phone conversations without any proof that a terrorist is using the phone and can conduct secret searches of your property. The law will still allow the government to send a letter to your bank, Internet Service Provider, insurance company, or any other business demanding

---

4 Less than a week after the attacks, President Bush visited a Washington mosque and assured those gathered there—while speaking to the whole of America as well—that the United States would not tolerate those who try to intimidate Muslims. "The face of terrorists is not the true faith of Islam. That's not what Islam is all about. Islam is peace."

information about you. . . . A government official can still forbid a business from telling anyone that records have been obtained, although this gag would last for an initial one-year period rather than indefinitely. However, the gag can be renewed. . . . Finally, the Bush Administration has magnanimously[5] agreed not to look at your library borrowing records, although this agreement makes it easier for them to find out what Web sites you visit while at the library.

The USA PATRIOT Act and other government policies put into place in response to 9/11 terrorist attacks severely impacted the civil rights of the Muslim community in America in a variety of ways. Discrimination against Muslims has been institutionalized[6] through the USA PATRIOT Act and other legislations. Muslims in schools, the workplace, airports, and encounters with police and other government agencies experienced incidents in which they were singled out because of their religious and ethnic identity.

New laws have also affected donations to the American Muslim charity organizations due to the lack of assurance that donors will be protected if any charity organization [is] later deemed by the government to be a terrorist organization. A fundamental problem is that even those American Muslim charities who follow the government's "best practices" guidelines to the letter do not receive any assurances that they will be safe. With major American Muslim charities—Holy Land Foundation for Relief and Development, Global Relief Foundation, Benevolence International Foundation, and Islamic American Relief Agency—shut down by the government over accusations of ties to terrorist groups and several prominent Muslim donors now indicted or detained, American Muslims are scared to do anything that might bring scrutiny from the FBI—and that includes donating to Islamic charities.

The administration, while shutting down the Muslim charity organizations using new powers under the USA PATRIOT Act, filed no criminal charges against these organizations, nor were they officially designated terrorist supporters. Law enforcement officials simply froze their assets and seized their property "pending an investigation" without producing any evidence, as authorized by the Act. Consequently, the burden of proof has been shifted to the organizations, which must prove

---

5 **magnanimously:** generously. Stark was speaking ironically.
6 **institutionalized:** made part of a well-established system

their innocence even though, in many cases, the government has not specified wrongdoing. Moreover, they must do this without access to their own documents, computers, records, or other materials that might make their case.

Muslim non-immigrants nationwide were jailed indefinitely over minor visa violations that in the past would have been ignored, and about 13,000, who went for INS[7] Special Registration voluntarily, faced deportation. The Justice Department's inspector general issued a scathing[8] report in April 2003 on the handling of 762 detainees held after September 11 under suspicion of having terrorist ties. It found "significant problems" with the treatment of some and uncovered evidence that family members and lawyers were not told where the men were taken.

The California Senate Report of March 2004 on the impact of the USA PATRIOT Act highlighted the plight of the Muslim community in the State of California, which has a substantial concentration of the Muslim population. The 82-page report—titled The PATRIOT Act, Other Post-9/11 Enforcement Powers and The Impact on California's Muslim Communities—pointed out that the Muslim community has taken the brunt of the PATRIOT Act and other federal powers applied in the aftermath of the 9/11 terrorist attacks. The measures created a fear that gripped the Muslim community in California and elsewhere following federal sweeps, round-ups, and detentions of innocent Muslims, who had neither terrorist intentions nor any connection to terrorist organizations, said the report, drawn up at the request of Senator Liz Figueroa (D-Fremont).

Congressman Pete Stark spoke for millions of Americans when he said while joining fellow San Francisco Bay Area Representatives George Miller, Barbara Lee, Mike Honda, Lynn Woolsey and Sam Farr in introducing the legislation to repeal provisions of the USA PATRIOT Act: "Having the honor of representing one of the most culturally diverse districts in the nation, I am keenly aware of the effects of the PATRIOT Act. Many of my constituents, especially those who are Arab and Muslim Americans, are afraid of losing their rights and being racially profiled and harassed by the government. . . . Perhaps worst of all, Attorney General

---

7   **INS:** Immigration and Naturalization Service, now called United States Citizenship and Immigration Services

8   **scathing:** bitterly critical. The report did, however, recognize "monumental challenges" facing the Department of Justice and recognized their dedicated work.

Ashcroft has wrongly singled out thousands of Americans of Arab, Middle Eastern, and South Asian descent for questioning and, in some cases, indefinite detainment."

The bill, titled the "Benjamin Franklin True Patriot Act,"[9] was introduced on September 24, 2003, in the House by Congressman Dennis J. Kucinich, the only presidential candidate [in the 2004 race] who voted against the USA PATRIOT Act. The True Patriot Act envisaged[10] repeal of a number of USA PATRIOT Act sections, including sections 441 and 442 related to the detention and deportation of non-citizens without meaningful judicial review. While introducing the True Patriot Act, Kucinich told the House: "Twenty-four months after the September 11th attacks, this nation has undergone a dramatic political change, leading to an unprecedented assault on the United States Constitution and the Bill of Rights."

Since its enactment, the USA PATRIOT Act has come under severe criticism in a variety of quarters. The Act's popularity waned to the point that the House of Representatives, on July 22, 2003, voted with bipartisan[11] support to cut off funds for enforcement of a key section—one that allows the FBI to enter and search private premises without showing the occupant a warrant or notifying the occupant that the place was searched, until some indeterminate time in the future. Other bills proposed outright repeal of several sections of the act, including allowing indefinite detention without trial.

There is a growing concern among the masses about the impact of the USA PATRIOT Act on their civil rights. As of August 11, 2006, 407 communities had passed resolutions calling for repeal of or otherwise faulting the USA PATRIOT Act, finding that certain provisions violate civil rights guaranteed by the Constitution. Moreover eight statewide resolutions were passed in Alaska, California, Colorado, Hawaii, Idaho, Maine, Montana, and Vermont. These communities represented approximately 85 million people who opposed sections of the USA PATRIOT Act. . . .

U.S. history is replete with the rollback of individual freedoms in times of national crisis. Many of these rollbacks and their consequences

---

9 The Act was named for Benjamin Franklin's famous remark, "Those who would give up Essential Liberty, to purchase a little temporary Safety, deserve neither Liberty nor Safety."

10 **envisaged:** laid out the possibility of

11 **bipartisan:** from both political parties

had disturbing results. McCarthyism[12] is one example. Perhaps the most stark example is the ordering of over 110,000 Japanese Americans to detention camps during World War II. The U.S. Supreme court failed to prevent or correct these national disgraces in a timely manner.

Fred Korematsu, a 22-year old loyal Japanese-American citizen by birth, who violated President Roosevelt's executive order by not going to an internment camp, challenged the constitutionality of the internment of an entire ethnic population class. In the landmark judgment the Supreme Court in 1944 held that Korematsu's constitutional freedoms were not violated and found him guilty. More than 41 years after his internment, in 1983, Korematsu [successfully] appealed his conviction [, which the judge said was] based on false, misleading, and racially biased information. In 1988 Congress passed legislation apologizing for the internments and awarded each survivor $20,000. . . .

Use of the USA PATRIOT Act in Criminal Cases

The Bush administration, which call[ed] the USA PATRIOT Act the most essential tool in fighting terrorists, was using the law with increasing frequency in many criminal investigations that have little or no connection to terrorism. . . . For instance, the ability to secure nationwide warrants to obtain e-mail and electronic evidence "has proved invaluable in several sensitive non-terrorism investigations," including the tracking of an unidentified fugitive and an investigation into a computer hacker who stole a company's trade secrets, [a Justice Department] report said.

Such use of the law confirms the belief of many that the administration [had] misled the public, using terrorism as a guise to pursue broader goals. Harvard Professor Gary Orfield got to the heart of the matter when he said: "The loss of civil rights often begins with the reduction of rights in a time of crisis, for a minority that has become the scapegoat for a problem facing the nation. The situation can become particularly explosive in a time of national tragedy or war. But when civil rights for one group of Americans are threatened and the disappearance of those rights [is] accepted, it becomes a potential threat to many others." This resonates very well with what the civil rights groups have been advocating in the post-9/11 era.

---

12 **McCarthyism:** A campaign against alleged communists in the U.S. government and other institutions during the Cold War under Senator Joseph McCarthy. See pages 24–26.

IN DEFENSE OF THE PATRIOT ACT

HEATHER MAC DONALD

In the editorial that follows, from the August 22, 2003, issue of the Washington Post, *a political commentator addresses some of the same criticisms of the USA PATRIOT Act that Ghazali raises in his report. (See pages 91–96.) Her perspective, however, is sharply different from his.*

The recent indictment[1] of a would-be arms merchant connected to al-Qaeda is only the latest reminder that the threat of terrorism is as urgent as ever. Yet many among the political and opinion elites act as if America is more at risk from the Bush administration's efforts to thwart future terror attacks than from the attackers themselves. Hardly a day passes without a well-publicized denunciation[2] of the government's alleged assault on civil liberties. Cities and counties across the country are declaring themselves "civil liberties safe zones," and a barrage[3] of bills in Congress seeks to repeal sections of the USA PATRIOT Act, the anti-terrorism law passed after 9/11, on the ground that it violates constitutional rights.

The American Civil Liberties Union recently filed a lawsuit in a Michigan federal court against the most frequent target of civil libertarian[4] ire—the Patriot Act's business records provision. The rhetoric[5] surrounding this provision, also known as Section 215, has been alarmist,[6] to say the least. In an editorial applauding the ACLU's action, *The Cleveland Plain Dealer,* for example, called the measure the "seedstock of a police state."

---

1 **indictment:** a formal accusation of a serious crime
2 **denunciation:** condemnation; severe criticism
3 **barrage:** bombardment
4 **civil libertarian:** one who advocates for civil liberties, believing the government's power and involvement in people's lives should be as small and unobtrusive as possible
5 **rhetoric:** language of debate and argument
6 **alarmist:** exaggerated and creating needless worry

WARRANTLESS WIRE TAPS

ONLINE MONITORING

BUSINESS RECORD DRAGNETS

LIBERTY

PRIVATE PROPERTY SEARCHES

ELECTRONIC SURVEILLANCE

DOMESTIC SPYING

PATRIOT ACT

Mike Keefe THE DENVER POST 7-1-11   www.caglecartoons.com

Section 215 allows the FBI to obtain documents in third-party hands if they are relevant to a terrorism investigation. According to the ACLU, this power allows the FBI to "spy on a person because they don't like the books she reads, or because . . . she wrote a letter to the editor that criticized government policy."

The charge is baseless. To begin with, it ignores the fact that the FBI can do nothing under Section 215 without the approval of a federal court. Let's say the FBI has received a tip that al-Qaeda sympathizers have taken scuba lessons in preparation for an attack on Navy destroyers off the California coast. Under 215, the bureau could seek a court order for local dive school records to see if any terror suspects had recently enrolled.

The key phrase here is "seek a court order." It is inconceivable that the court that oversees espionage and counterterrorism investigations will approve a records request made because the FBI doesn't "like the books" someone reads, or "because she wrote a letter to the editor that criticized government policy," as the ACLU claims.

The ACLU also argues that Section 215 violates the Fourth Amendment right to privacy. But like it or not, once you've disclosed information to someone else, the Constitution no longer protects it. This diffuse[7]-it-and-lose-it rule applies to library borrowing and Web surfing as well, however

---

7 **diffuse:** spread around

much librarians may claim otherwise. By publicly borrowing library books, patrons forfeit any constitutional protections they may have had in their reading habits.

Another ACLU attack on 215 uses the tactic of ignoring legal precedent.[8] Grand juries investigating a crime have always been able to subpoena[9] the very items covered by 215—including library records and Internet logs—without seeking a warrant or indeed any judicial approval at all. Section 215 merely gives anti-terror investigators the same access to such records as criminal grand juries, with the added protection of judicial oversight.

The administration's opponents reply that grand-jury subpoenas are preferable, because they can be contested in court and are not always confidential, as are 215 orders. But these differences are fully justified by the distinction between preempting[10] terrorism and prosecuting crime. Speed and secrecy are essential to uncovering a terror plot before it climaxes. The perils of unnecessary delay were made clear in the Zacarias Moussaoui[11] case, when Justice Department bureaucrats, virtually mummified by red tape, forbade Minneapolis FBI agents from searching the al-Qaeda operative's computer in the weeks before 9/11.

Critics of the administration also decry[12] the Patriot Act's provision for delaying notice of a search—the so-called "sneak-and-peak" rule—as an outrageous power grab by the government. The Patriot Act naysayers don't tell you that there is nothing new about this power at all: Judges have long allowed the government to delay notice of a search if notifying the target would risk witness intimidation, destruction of evidence or flight from prosecution. The Patriot Act merely codifies[13] existing case law into one national standard.

In introducing a bill [in July, 2003] to amend Section 215, Sen. Russell Feingold (D-Wis.) alleged that Americans had become "afraid to read books, terrified into silence." Were that ever the case, it would be thanks to the misinformation spread by advocates and politicians, not because of any real threat posed by the Bush administration's war on terror.

---

8 **legal precedent:** court cases that have come before and addressed relevant aspects of the law

9 **subpoena:** issue a summoning order to appear in court

10 **preempting:** stopping before it happens

11 **Zacarias Moussaouti:** a French citizen convicted as a conspirator in the 9/11 attacks.

12 **decry:** publicly denounce or oppose

13 **codifies:** establishes in a systematic code or law

MIRANDA FOR JUVENILES

JUSTICE SONIA SOTOMAYOR

If you have seen any television show about the police, you will recognize what has come to be called the Miranda warning: "You have the right to remain silent. Anything you say or do can and will be held against you in a court of law. You have the right to speak to an attorney. If you cannot afford an attorney, one will be appointed for you. Do you understand these rights as they have been read to you?" This warning came out of a 1966 Supreme Court case, Miranda v. Arizona, *in which the judges ruled that to protect a suspect's Fifth Amendment right to avoid self-incrimination, the warning had to be read when a suspect was being held by the police before any interrogation could begin. If suspects are not so warned, their statements and even confessions are not admissible as evidence in court. In 2011, the Supreme Court considered the application of the Miranda warning to juveniles in a case involving a young boy known only by his initials J.D.B. to protect his identity. Justice Sonia Sotomayor, named to the court in 2009, wrote the opinion, which was released on June 16, 2011. Excerpts from the opinion follow.*

This case presents the question whether the age of a child subjected to police questioning is relevant to the custody[1] analysis of *Miranda v. Arizona* (1966). It is beyond dispute that children will often feel bound to submit to police questioning when an adult in the same circumstances would feel free to leave. Seeing no reason for police officers or courts to blind themselves to that commonsense reality, we hold that a child's age properly informs[2] the *Miranda* custody analysis. . . .

Petitioner J. D. B. was a 13-year-old, seventh-grade student attending class at Smith Middle School in Chapel Hill, North Carolina, when he was removed from his classroom by a uniformed police officer, escorted to a closed-door conference room, and questioned by police for at least half an hour.

---

1 **custody:** In this context, custody refers to being officially held by the police.
2 **informs:** is relevant to

This was the second time that police questioned J. D. B. in the span of a week. Five days earlier, two home break-ins occurred, and various items were stolen. Police stopped and questioned J. D. B. after he was seen behind a residence in the neighborhood where the crimes occurred. That same day, police also spoke to J. D. B.'s grandmother—his legal guardian—as well as his aunt.

Police later learned that a digital camera matching the description of one of the stolen items had been found at J. D. B.'s middle school and seen in J. D. B.'s possession. Investigator DiCostanzo, the juvenile investigator with the local police force who had been assigned to the case, went to the school to question J. D. B. Upon arrival, DiCostanzo informed the uniformed police officer on detail to the school (a so-called school resource officer), the assistant principal, and an administrative intern that he was there to question J. D. B. about the break-ins. Although DiCostanzo asked the school administrators to verify J. D. B.'s date of birth, address, and parent contact information from school records, neither the police officers nor the school administrators contacted J. D. B.'s grandmother.

The uniformed officer interrupted J. D. B.'s afternoon social studies class, removed J. D. B. from the classroom, and escorted him to a school conference room. There, J. D. B. was met by DiCostanzo, the assistant principal, and the administrative intern. The door to the conference room was closed. With the two police officers and the two administrators present, J. D. B. was questioned for the next 30 to 45 minutes. Prior to the commencement of questioning, J. D. B. was given neither *Miranda* warnings nor the opportunity to speak to his grandmother. Nor was he informed that he was free to leave the room.

Questioning began with small talk—discussion of sports and J. D. B.'s family life. DiCostanzo asked, and J. D. B. agreed, to discuss the events of the prior weekend. Denying any wrongdoing, J. D. B. explained that he had been in the neighborhood where the crimes occurred because he was seeking work mowing lawns. DiCostanzo pressed J. D. B. for additional detail about his efforts to obtain work; asked J. D. B. to explain a prior incident, when one of the victims returned home to find J. D. B. behind her house; and confronted J. D. B. with the stolen camera. The assistant principal urged J. D. B. to "do the right thing," warning J. D. B. that "the truth always comes out in the end."

Eventually, J. D. B. asked whether he would "still be in trouble" if he returned the "stuff." In response, DiCostanzo explained that return of the stolen items would be helpful, but "this thing is going to court" regardless. ("[W]hat's done is done[;] now you need to help yourself by making it right.") DiCostanzo then warned that he may need to seek a secure custody order if he believed that J. D. B. would continue to break into other homes. When J. D. B. asked what a secure custody order was, DiCostanzo explained that "it's where you get sent to juvenile detention before court."

After learning of the prospect of juvenile detention, J. D. B. confessed that he and a friend were responsible for the break-ins. DiCostanzo only then informed J. D. B. that he could refuse to answer the investigator's questions and that he was free to leave. Asked whether he understood, J. D. B. nodded and provided further detail, including information about the location of the stolen items. Eventually J. D. B. wrote a statement, at DiCostanzo's request. When the bell rang indicating the end of the schoolday, J. D. B. was allowed to leave to catch the bus home.

Two juvenile petitions were filed against J. D. B., each alleging one count of breaking and entering and one count of larceny.[3] J. D. B.'s public defender moved to suppress[4] his statements and the evidence [they offered], arguing that suppression was necessary because J. D. B. had been "interrogated by police in a custodial setting without being afforded *Miranda* warning[s]," and because his statements were involuntary. . . . After a suppression hearing at which DiCostanzo and J. D. B. testified, the trial court denied the motion, deciding that J. D. B. was not in custody at the time of the schoolhouse interrogation and that his statements were voluntary . . . [and he was found guilty based on his admission. The North Carolina Court of Appeals upheld this ruling, arguing that J. D. B. was not in custody when he confessed and "declin[ing] to extend the test for custody to include consideration of the age . . . of an individual subjected to questioning by police."]

[Sotomayor next reviews the cases that have shaped the courts' understanding of what it means for a suspect to be "in custody." Only when a suspect can be considered in custody is the Miranda warning required. She quotes from a 1995 finding: "Two discrete inquiries are essential to the determination [of whether a suspect is in custody]: first, what were the circumstances surrounding the interrogation; and second, given those circumstances, would a reasonable person have felt he or she was at liberty to terminate the interrogation and leave."

---

3 **larceny:** theft
4 **suppress:** hold back; not use as evidence

She goes on to summarize the arguments the State provides that a child's age should not be a relevant factor in determining custody. She then shows why the Court is not convinced by those arguments.]

The State and its *amici*[5] contend that a child's age has no place in the custody analysis, no matter how young the child subjected to police questioning. We cannot agree. In some circumstances, a child's age "would have affected how a reasonable person" in the suspect's position "would perceive his or her freedom to leave." That is, a reasonable child subjected to police questioning will sometimes feel pressured to submit when a reasonable adult would feel free to go. . . .

In fact, in many cases involving juvenile suspects, the custody analysis would be nonsensical absent[6] some consideration of the suspect's age. This case is a prime example. Were the court precluded from taking J. D. B.'s youth into account, it would be forced to evaluate the circumstances present here through the eyes of a reasonable person of average years. In other words, how would a reasonable adult understand his situation, after being removed from a seventh-grade social studies class by a uniformed school resource officer; being encouraged by his assistant principal to "do the right thing"; and being warned by a police investigator of the prospect of juvenile detention and separation from his guardian and primary caretaker? To describe such an inquiry is to demonstrate its absurdity. Neither officers nor courts can reasonably evaluate the effect of objective circumstances that, by their nature, are specific to children without accounting for the age of the child subjected to those circumstances.

[Justice Sotomayor then cites previous court rulings that argue against the state's position that a juvenile defendant's age is not relevant, or that it blurs the clarity of the definition of custody.]

The question remains whether J. D. B. was in custody when police interrogated him. We remand[7] for the state courts to address that question, this time taking account of all of the relevant circumstances of the interrogation, including J. D. B.'s age at the time. The judgment of the North Carolina Supreme Court is reversed, and the case is remanded for proceedings not inconsistent with this opinion.

It is so ordered.

---

5 **amici:** parties not directly involved in the case who have submitted supporting documents

6 **absent:** without

7 **remand:** send a case back

Impartial Jurors, Impartial Juries

Newton R. Minow

The Sixth Amendment guarantees that the accused have a right to a trial by an impartial jury. But what makes a jury impartial? Mass media specialist Newton Minow considers the effect of the omnipresent media and Internet on the impartiality of juries.

If, after sleeping for several hundred years, Rip van Winkle woke up today and walked into a courtroom, he would be surprised by the way we pick juries.

In 1807, when Aaron Burr[1] was on trial for treason, Burr's lawyer said to the court, "We can't get a fair jury because there has been too much publicity. We don't want anybody who knows anything about the case."

The argument went to Chief Justice John Marshall, who said, "Well, that's impossible. We don't want to discourage citizens from being well-informed. They can be on the jury provided they say they will be fair and decide the case on what they hear in the courtroom."

Through the years, we've changed that approach, but little else in the legal system is terribly different from what Rip van Winkle would have found 200 years ago. If he stepped outside the courtroom, however, he wouldn't believe what he saw. He would discover radio, television, cable, satellites, telephones, computers, wireless communication, faxes. He would even discover the Internet. There's been a revolution outside the courtroom.

Today, most people in the United States get most of their information from radio and television rather than from print (although 64 percent of the population does read newspapers). The radio is on for most people more than three hours a day. Television is on as much as seven hours a day. We now have a media-saturated society. . . .

---

1 **Aaron Burr:** Third Vice President of the United States, serving under Thomas Jefferson. Burr was acquitted on the treason charges.

I think it's madness, in today's mass media society, to search for jurors who know nothing. . . .

Just as Chief Justice Marshall decided in 1807, we have to recognize the difference between an impartial juror and an impartial jury. The whole concept of having 12 people on a jury is to bring people of diverse backgrounds and perspectives into one room to decide a case. It is not to find 12 people who are all the same.

A Jury of Peers

The origins of the jury system are in 11th-century England. The concept was that people were entitled to a jury of their peers. At that time, a peer meant someone who knew the accused, someone who lived in the neighborhood and knew who was a liar and who would tell the truth. If the potential juror was a stranger, he could not serve on a jury. Somehow, over the centuries, we turned that upside down.

In fact, we've turned the tables. We now ask jurors more about themselves than they may learn in the courtroom about the parties in the dispute. When a person is called for jury duty, we give him or her a massive questionnaire. In some cases, the questions can go on for 100 pages.

[In 1995], a woman named Dianna Brandborg was called for jury duty in Texas and given a series of questions to answer, such as, What is your income? What is your religion? What books do you read? What are your favorite television programs? Have you ever been divorced?

She finally got upset and said, "I'm entitled to some privacy. These questions are nobody's business but my own." The judge said, "OK, lady, you're going to jail for contempt," and he put her in prison.[2] . . .

Unsullied Justice

In 1871, Mark Twain attended a trial in Virginia and witnessed the jury selection. He wrote:

> I remember one of those sorrowful farces in Virginia, which we call a jury trial. A noted desperado killed Mr. B., a good citizen, in the most wanton and cold-blooded way. Of course, the papers were full of it; all men capable of reading read about it; and, of course, all men not deaf and dumb and idiotic talked about it.

---

2 Brandborg never had to serve her 3-day sentence or pay her $200 fine. Her attorney immediately appealed the ruling and a year and half later the case was resolved in her favor.

A minister, intelligent, esteemed and well respected, a merchant of high character and known probity, a mining superintendent of intelligence and unblemished reputation, a quartz mill owner of excellent standing were all questioned in the same way, and all were set aside from the jury.

Each said public talk and the newspaper reports had not biased his mind, but that sworn testimony would overthrow any previously formed opinion and would enable him to render a verdict without prejudice and in accordance with the facts.

But such men could not be trusted with the case. Ignoramuses alone could mete out unsullied justice. . . .

We live in a world where the mass media are omnipresent. As we seek to reconcile the courts and the mass media, we ought to start by ending the practice where defendants and prosecutors know more about the jurors than the jury will ever know about the prosecutors and defendants.

Emmett Till

James A. Emanuel

Emmett Till, an African American boy from Chicago, was killed at age 14 while visiting relatives in Mississippi in 1955. Unaccustomed to the profound racial barriers in the South, Emmett had whistled at a white married woman. The woman's husband, Roy Bryant, and his half-brother J. W. Milan, brutally beat and murdered the young boy for his unforgiveable breech of custom. They tossed him in the Tallahatchie River with a fan from a cotton gin wrapped around his neck, tied with barbed wire, to weigh him down. An all-white jury acquitted Bryant and Milam, who shortly after the trial confessed to the murder in an interview published in Look *magazine. They knew they could not be charged for the same crime again because of the double jeopardy clause of the Fifth Amendment. However, the murder of Emmett Till and the verdict by the all-white jury was a turning point in the momentum of the civil rights movement, rallying outraged Americans to take an unmovable stand for justice. The story of Emmett Till was told again and again in the songs and poetry of America. Fifty-two years after his murder, Tallahatchie County issued a formal apology to Till's family: "We the citizens of Tallahatchie County recognize that the Emmett Till case was a terrible miscarriage of justice. We state candidly and with deep regret the failure to effectively pursue justice. We wish to say to the family of Emmett Till that we are profoundly sorry for what was done in this community to your loved one."*

I hear a whistling
Through the water.
Little Emmett
Won't be still.
He keeps floating
Round the darkness,
Edging through

The silent chill.
Tell me, please,
That bedtime story
Of the fairy
River Boy
Who swims forever,
Deep in treasures,
Necklaced in
A coral toy.

In an electrifying moment during the trial of Bryant and Milam, Mose Wright, Emmett Till's great uncle, identified the men who had come for Emmett that terrible night. Observers called his act historic, since African Americans had traditionally been intimidated into silence about white injustice.

RESPONDING TO CLUSTER THREE

WHY ARE SUSPECTS' RIGHTS IMPORTANT?

Critical Thinking Skill INTEGRATING MULTIMEDIA INFORMATION

1. In the article "Atoms vs. Bits: Your Phone in the Eyes of the Law," to what objects are cell phones compared in court cases dealing with search and seizure laws? Which analogy or comparison best supports the author's position on cell phone searches? Explain your own point of view on the issue, supporting it with details from the selection and the graph on page 85.

2. Analyze how Orwell's word choice and tone support the theme of invasion of privacy in the excerpt from *Nineteen Eighty-Four*. Then view a scene from a movie version of the novel (available on YouTube). Use the chart to document specific examples of evocative description or visuals. Which format do you find more effective, and why?

Theme: Invasion of privacy	
Selection from book	Scene from movie

3. Analyze the poems "The Work of Brothers" and "Emmett Till." Identify language and structure that seem particularly effective in conveying the emotions surrounding these acts of injustice. Extend your experience by studying the photo on page 90 and listening to "Death of Emmett Till" by Bob Dylan.

4. Contrast "The Civil Rights of American Muslims After 9/11" and "In Defense of the Patriot Act." Analyze both pieces by identifying the writers' central claims and how they support their claims with reasons, examples, and evidence. Identify where the writers interpret facts differently.

5. Explain the Supreme Court ruling from "Miranda for Juveniles." Summarize the reasons the Court gave for its ruling. Make an inference about how this case might change the way school police officers interrogate students suspected of crimes.

6. How does the section **A Jury of Peers** from "Impartial Jurors, Impartial Juries" fit into the writer's argument? What examples from recent history might present a valid counterargument to Minow's claims?

Writing Activity: Integrate Information in a Multimedia Presentation

Create a multimedia presentation that alerts people to the helpful or harmful ways that technology has influenced the pursuit of justice. Use information from this cluster as well as your own research. Include images, words, and/or music. Consider publishing your presentation on YouTube or other appropriate sites.

A Strong Presentation

- communicates a main idea
- develops the main idea using examples and evidence
- uses visual and sound elements to reinforce the main idea and evoke an emotional response

CLUSTER FOUR

Thinking on Your Own

Critical Thinking Skill
INTEGRATING SOURCES OF INFORMATION

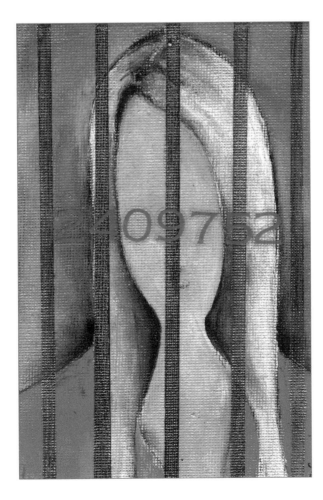

TINKER CASE GUIDES COURT AS STUDENT'S PARODY OF PRINCIPAL IS RULED PROTECTED SPEECH

BETH HAWKINS

All the selections in Cluster Four are presented as paired readings, and all address issues of special relevance for young people. The first pair examines the issue of free speech for students, looking at two landmark Supreme Court cases that helped establish what kinds of speech are and are not free in a school setting. In the first selection, a journalist reviews the 1969 Tinker v. Des Moines *case and shows how it was applied in a more recent case involving a fake MySpace page.*

In 1965, a 13-year-old Iowa girl by the name of Mary Beth Tinker wore a black armband to school in protest of the Vietnam War and in defiance of a school-board policy enacted specifically to ward off the display.

Mary Beth Tinker and her brother John

She was also defying her mother and father, Methodist ministers, Freedom Riders, and her principled inspiration, but also parents who would just as soon not borrow trouble.

As expected, Tinker, her brother, and another student were suspended. After they were allowed back in school, they wore black for the rest of the year in protest.

They also came to the attention of the American Civil Liberties Union, which waged a four-year court battle on their behalf that culminated in *Tinker v. Des Moines*, a landmark U.S. Supreme Court decision barring public school officials from censoring student speech unless it disrupts the educational process.

A Guide For Four Decades

Students, seven of the nine justices famously held, do not "shed their constitutional rights to freedom of speech or expression at the schoolhouse gate." In the four decades since, the opinion has guided decisions on everything from school uniform policies to the rights of LGBT[1] students.

Tinker, for her part, is active in directing the Marshall-Brennan Constitutional Literacy Project at American University, which mobilizes law students to teach courses on constitutional law and juvenile justice at public schools.

As such, it's reasonable to assume that she took note of the most recent *Tinker* progeny,[2] handed down Monday [June 13, 2011] by the U.S. District Court of Appeals for the Third Circuit. And it's reasonable to assume that she stood firm behind the principles at stake in *Layshock v. Hermitage School District*.

She would be forgiven if she rolled her eyes at the speech in question.

A fake MySpace 'profile' In 2005, 17-year-old Pennsylvania resident Justin Layshock signed on to a computer at his grandmother's house and created a fake MySpace "profile" for Eric Trosch, principal of Hickory High School. In it, he described the principal as a "big steroid freak" who keeps a "big keg behind [his] desk" and fears "students laughing at [him]."

"Justin created the profile by giving bogus answers to survey questions taken from various templates that were designed to assist in creating a profile," the appeals court summarized. "The survey included questions about favorite shoes, weaknesses, fears, one's idea of a 'perfect pizza,' bedtime, etc. All of Justin's answers were based on a theme of 'big,' because Trosch is apparently a large man."

Layshock would later describe the profile as a parody, never mind that it has much more in common with "Beavis and Butthead" than, say, "The Colbert Report."[3] (Which he apparently watches; perhaps he has since learned something about the incisive[4] potential of the parody.)

The humor held enough appeal for teenage boys that three classmates copied Layshock, except with lewder and more explicit content.

---

1 **LGBT:** Lesbian, Gay, Bisexual, and Transgender
2 **progeny:** offspring
3 "Beavis and Butthead" is an animated TV show in which the title characters are known for somewhat low-level humor. "The Colbert Report," hosted by Stephen Colbert, who parodies a conservative broadcaster, is a satirical look at political commentary on television.
4 **incisive:** cutting; biting

Predictably, word of the pranks spread "like wildfire" and Layshock & Co. were busted.

Layshock was the only one of the four who came clean. The copycats were not punished.

Senior was suspended and transferred In Layshock's case, the principal called the police and considered a defamation lawsuit,[5] but ended up suspending the senior for 10 days, transferring him to an alternative learning center normally reserved for students who can't function in a normal classroom, barring him from extracurricular activities and from graduation ceremonies.

Layshock's family sued and on Monday [June 13, 2011], a federal appeals court sided with them, articulating much the same reasoning the high court set forth in *Tinker*: The speech in question is constitutionally protected.

"Because the School District concedes that Justin's profile did not cause disruption in the school, we do not think that the First Amendment can tolerate the School District stretching its authority into Justin's grandmother's home and reaching Justin while he is sitting at her computer after school in order to punish him for the expressive conduct that he engaged in there," the court found.

"We realize, of course, that it is now well established that *Tinker*'s 'schoolhouse gate' is not constructed solely of the bricks and mortar surrounding the school yard. Nevertheless, the concept of the 'school yard' is not without boundaries and the reach of school authorities is not without limits."

Unlikely to disrupt education process That the speech "reached inside the school" didn't matter, because it was unlikely to disrupt the education process—unlike an Internet post threatening a teacher or fellow student or one that urged students to act out. Layshock's misbehavior was in fact dealt with at home. His parents grounded him and took away his computer privileges.

And if that doesn't seem like punishment enough, consider this: Wherever he is, Layshock, who is now probably 23 and turning his sights to such niceties as graduation or professional school or a job, must go forward knowing exactly what a mere Google search of his name will reveal.

---

5 **defamation lawsuit:** a suit claiming that one's character has been defamed, or damaged

STUDENT SPEECH CAN BE RESTRICTED

CHIEF JUSTICE JOHN ROBERTS

This second reading on the question of free speech for students is an excerpt from the opinion written by Chief Justice John Roberts in the 2007 case of Morse v. Frederick. *Like many cases that make it to the Supreme Court, this case involves language that many might find offensive. In fact, the judges in this case found that the language was of such a nature that the school superintendent's suspension of the offending student did not violate his First Amendment rights. What made his speech different from the expression the Court protected in the Tinker case?*

At a school-sanctioned and school-supervised event, a high school principal saw some of her students unfurl a large banner conveying a message she reasonably regarded as promoting illegal drug use. Consistent with established school policy prohibiting such messages at school events, the principal directed the students to take down the banner. One student—among those who had brought the banner to the event—refused to do so. The principal confiscated the banner and later suspended the student. The Ninth Circuit held that the principal's actions violated the First Amendment, and that the student could sue the principal for damages.

Our cases make clear that students do not "shed their constitutional rights to freedom of speech or expression at the schoolhouse gate" [*Tinker v. Des Moines Independent Community School District* (1969)]. At the same time, we have held that "the constitutional rights of students in public school are not automatically coextensive with the rights of adults in other settings" [*Bethel School District No. 403 v. Fraser* (1986)], and that the rights of students "must be 'applied in light of the special characteristics of the school environment'" [*Hazelwood School District v. Kuhlmeier* (1988) (quoting *Tinker*)]. Consistent with these principles, we hold that schools may take steps to safeguard those entrusted to their care from speech that can reasonably be regarded as encouraging illegal drug use. We conclude that the school officials in this case did not violate the First Amendment by confiscating the pro-drug banner and suspending the student responsible for it.

On January 24, 2002, the Olympic Torch Relay passed through Juneau, Alaska, on its way to the winter games in Salt Lake City, Utah. The torchbearers were to proceed along a street in front of Juneau-Douglas High School (JDHS) while school was in session. Petitioner Deborah Morse, the school principal, decided to permit staff and students to participate in the Torch Relay as an approved social event or class trip. Students were allowed to leave class to observe the relay from either side of the street. Teachers and administrative officials monitored the students' actions.

Respondent Joseph Frederick, a JDHS senior, was late to school that day. When he arrived, he joined his friends (all but one of whom were JDHS students) across the street from the school to watch the event. Not all the students waited patiently. Some became rambunctious, throwing plastic cola bottles and snowballs and scuffling with their classmates. As the torchbearers and camera crews passed by, Frederick and his friends unfurled a 14-foot banner bearing the phrase: "BONG HiTS 4 JESUS." The large banner was easily readable by the students on the other side of the street.

Principal Morse immediately crossed the street and demanded that the banner be taken down. Everyone but Frederick complied. Morse confiscated the banner and told Frederick to report to her office, where she suspended him for 10 days. Morse later explained that she told Frederick to take the banner down because she thought it encouraged illegal drug use, in violation of established school policy. Juneau School Board Policy No. 5520 states: "The Board specifically prohibits any assembly or public expression that . . . advocates the use of substances that are illegal to minors. . . ." In addition, Juneau School Board Policy No. 5850 subjects "[p]upils who participate in approved social events and class trips" to the same student conduct rules that apply during the regular school program. . . .

At the outset, we reject Frederick's argument that this is not a school speech case—as has every other authority to address the question. The event occurred during normal school hours. It was sanctioned by Principal Morse "as an approved social event or class trip," and the school district's rules expressly provide that pupils in "approved social events and class trips are subject to district rules for student conduct."

Teachers and administrators were interspersed among the students and charged with supervising them. The high school band and cheerleaders performed. Frederick, standing among other JDHS students across the street from the school, directed his banner toward the school, making it plainly visible to most students. Under these circumstances, we agree with the superintendent that Frederick cannot "stand in the midst of his fellow students, during school hours, at a school-sanctioned activity and claim he is not at school." There is some uncertainty at the outer boundaries as to when courts should apply school speech precedents, but not on these facts. . . .

The question thus becomes whether a principal may, consistent with the First Amendment, restrict student speech at a school event, when that speech is reasonably viewed as promoting illegal drug use. We hold that she may.

In *Tinker,* this Court made clear that "First Amendment rights, applied in light of the special characteristics of the school environment, are available to teachers and students." Tinker involved a group of high school students who decided to wear black armbands to protest the Vietnam War. School officials learned of the plan and then adopted a policy prohibiting students from wearing armbands. When several students nonetheless wore armbands to school, they were suspended. The students sued, claiming that their First Amendment rights had been violated, and this Court agreed.

Tinker held that student expression may not be suppressed unless school officials reasonably conclude that it will "materially and substantially disrupt the work and discipline of the school." The essential facts of *Tinker* are quite stark, implicating[1] concerns at the heart of the First Amendment. The students sought to engage in political speech, using the armbands to express their "disapproval of the Vietnam hostilities and their advocacy of a truce, to make their views known, and, by their example, to influence others to adopt them." Political speech, of

---

1 **implicating:** closely connecting

course, is "at the core of what the First Amendment is designed to protect" [*Virginia v. Black* (2003)]. The only interest the Court discerned underlying the school's actions was the "mere desire to avoid the discomfort and unpleasantness that always accompany an unpopular viewpoint," or "an urgent wish to avoid the controversy which might result from the expression" [*Tinker*]. That interest was not enough to justify banning "a silent, passive expression of opinion, unaccompanied by any disorder or disturbance.". . .

Drawing on the principles applied in our student speech cases, we have held in the Fourth Amendment context that "while children assuredly do not 'shed their constitutional rights . . . at the schoolhouse gate,' . . . the nature of those rights is what is appropriate for children in school" [*Vernonia School District v. Acton* (1995) (quoting *Tinker*)]. In particular, "the school setting requires some easing of the restrictions to which searches by public authorities are ordinarily subject" [*New Jersey v. T.L.O.* (1985)].

Even more to the point, these cases also recognize that deterring drug use by schoolchildren is an "important—indeed, perhaps compelling" interest [*Vernonia*]. Drug abuse can cause severe and permanent damage to the health and well-being of young people:

> School years are the time when the physical, psychological, and addictive effects of drugs are most severe. Maturing nervous systems are more critically impaired by intoxicants than mature ones are; childhood losses in learning are lifelong and profound; children grow chemically dependent more quickly than adults, and their record of recovery is depressingly poor. And of course the effects of a drug-infested school are visited not just upon the users, but upon the entire student body and faculty, as the educational process is disrupted.

Just five years ago, we wrote: "The drug abuse problem among our nation's youth has hardly abated since *Vernonia* was decided in 1995. In fact, evidence suggests that it has only grown worse" [*Board of Education v. Earls, 2002*].

The problem remains serious today. About half of American 12th graders have used an illicit drug, as have more than a third of 10th graders and about one-fifth of 8th graders. Nearly one in four 12th graders has used an illicit drug in the past month. Some 25% of high schoolers say that they have been offered, sold, or given an illegal drug on school property within the past year.

Congress has declared that part of a school's job is educating students about the dangers of illegal drug use. It has provided billions of dollars to support state and local drug prevention programs, and required that schools receiving federal funds under the Safe and Drug-Free Schools and Communities Act of 1994 certify that their drug prevention programs "convey a clear and consistent message that . . . the illegal use of drugs [is] wrong and harmful."

Thousands of school boards throughout the country—including JDHS—have adopted policies aimed at effectuating[2] this message. Those school boards know that peer pressure is perhaps "the single most important factor leading schoolchildren to take drugs," and that students are more likely to use drugs when the norms in school appear to tolerate such behavior [*Earls*]. Student speech celebrating illegal drug use at a school event, in the presence of school administrators and teachers, thus poses a particular challenge for school officials working to protect those entrusted to their care from the dangers of drug abuse.

The "special characteristics of the school environment" [*Tinker*], and the governmental interest in stopping student drug abuse—reflected in the policies of Congress and myriad school boards, including JDHS— allow schools to restrict student expression that they reasonably regard as promoting illegal drug use. *Tinker* warned that schools may not prohibit student speech because of "undifferentiated fear or apprehension of disturbance" or "a mere desire to avoid the discomfort and unpleasantness that always accompany an unpopular viewpoint." The danger here is far more serious and palpable.[3] The particular concern to prevent student drug abuse at issue here, embodied in established school policy, extends well beyond an abstract desire to avoid controversy. . . .

School principals have a difficult job, and a vitally important one. When Frederick suddenly and unexpectedly unfurled his banner, Morse had to decide to act—or not act—on the spot. It was reasonable for her to conclude that the banner promoted illegal drug use—in violation of established school policy—and that failing to act would send a powerful message to the students in her charge, including Frederick, about how serious the school was about the dangers of illegal drug use. The First Amendment does not require schools to tolerate at school events student expression that contributes to those dangers.

---

2 **effectuating**: putting into action
3 **palpable**: immediate; able to be touched

'WEBCAMGATE' SHOWS YOUTH ARE NOT APATHETIC ABOUT PRIVACY

MARIO RODRIGUEZ

The next two readings address the issue of students' privacy. The first story is from a Web site called "Visual Inquiry," hosted by the Annenberg School for Communication at the University of Pennsylvania. The purpose of "Visual Inquiry" is to explore "the transformations of visual media and their impact on society and culture." Webcams are an obvious example of a visual technology that has the potential to exert such a profound impact. This first story concerns the use of hidden Webcams on computers that schools have loaned to students to use at home.

Blake Robbins has the honor of being one of the first people on earth to be targeted by a covert[1] institutional campaign of webcam surveillance and expose it. It is a story so compelling that it has appeared in newspapers as far flung as the UK, Australia, and even Bangkok. It happened in the Lower Merion County School District, one of Pennsylvania's wealthiest, just outside of Philadelphia.

Blake Robbins, 15, was asked to visit Harriton High School Assistant Principal Lindy Matsko on November 11 [2009] in her office, whereupon Matsko accused Blake of "improper behavior in his home" and cited a photo surreptitiously taken on his laptop webcam. According to *The Philadelphia Inquirer* Matsko actually showed Blake a picture of himself in which he appeared to be taking drugs, but, according to Mark S. Haltzman, attorney for the Robbins family, this was just candy. In fact, it was Mike & Ike.[2]

What has now become "Webcamgate" has led to a class action lawsuit filed on February 11 [2010] by the parents and families of the school

---

1 **covert:** secret
2 **Mike & Ike:** fruit-flavored candies

district. According to information released by the district in the wake of this fiasco,[3] technicians at the school were authorized through a covert program by administrators (such as Matsko) to take pictures remotely using the built-in iSight webcams in the Apple laptop computers issued to students. Once activated on an individual laptop, the "Theft Tracker" software begins snapping photos and recording the computer's Internet location. The default setting was every 15 minutes.

The 42 photos in question (taken unbeknownst to the students and families) were snapped in fall of 2008 just after the laptops were loaned to kids, and after an incident during which half a dozen laptops were stolen from the locker room during gym class. What sounds particularly disturbing to critics of this incident, most likely, is the oft-quoted line from the lawsuit that many of the images snapped by the webcams "may consist of minors and their parents or friends in compromising or embarrassing positions" including "stages of undress."

Notice the "function creep" of the Apple laptops and their iSight cameras. According to an online definition from the Oxford University Press website, *function creep* is a noun that describes "the way in which information that has been collected for one limited purpose, is gradually allowed to be used for other purposes which people may not approve of." A more systemic example might be marketing companies that exploit public safety databases for advertising purposes. In the Harriton case, "function creep" has made the school's upper-middle class families the unwitting playground for an experiment with a new type of surveillance by virtue of the ubiquity[4] of new media.

As an EPIC [Electronic Privacy Information Center] representative put it, if the district thought what it was doing was right it wouldn't have discontinued the program after it was exposed. In fact the School District turned images taken by the program over to local police on at least two occasions to help track stolen laptops. The District even went so far as to set up a secure Web site for the police to access the pictures and other information. "Quite honestly, the police knew about these devices," said one lawyer involved in the case. "They were not in the dark about the fact that these computers were being tracked."

This story, and its aftermath, is probably not an isolated incident. Another case of student resistance to over-reaching school administrators

---

3 **fiasco:** complete failure
4 **ubiquity:** omnipresence; ability to be everywhere always

has been cited by Jen Weiss,[5] who described a spontaneous protest involving 1,500 students on Sept. 21, 2005, at Baldwin High School in the Bronx, [a borough of New York City] during which students, disgruntled[6] with draconian[7] surveillance measures and bans on personal electronic devices that the school administration had unveiled without consent, marched to the borough superintendent's office at Fordham Plaza and negotiated with police officials. The terms

that were reached were not long lasting, but Weiss describes strategies of resistance to combat the "double bind" of students made to conform to the rules of security officials and subject to humiliation before peers. Weiss claims that these strategies . . . of students are actually relatively invisible micropractices,[8] but that with the ubiquity of surveillance devices they may be some of the few means of resistance left to youth.

There is a seeming irony in such stories of students' resistance to ubiquitous surveillance of their behavior. In recent years, media critics have been lamenting young people's seeming lack of concern about personal privacy, an attitude that is supposedly manifested through the posting of overly revealing personal information on Facebook and other social networking sites. Cultural commentators have also drawn connections between acceptance of surveillance, on the one hand, and the increasing popularity of self-revealing reality shows, on the other.

However, as we see in the Harriton and Baldwin cases, perhaps we need to be a bit more skeptical about such broad generalizations. Young people's attitudes towards privacy and surveillance are probably a lot more complicated than might we know. . . .

---

5 Jennifer Weiss wrote a dissertation titled "Under the Radar: School Surveillance and Youth Resistance," for her Ph.D. from City University of New York.

6 **disgruntled:** angry and dissatisfied

7 **draconian:** harsh

8 **micropractices:** very small things that can be done

SAFE SCHOOLS, CELL PHONES, AND THE FOURTH AMENDMENT

BERNARD JAMES

While "Webcamgate" resolved the constitutionality question in favor of the students, the landmark case New Jersey v. TLO *was decided in favor of the school. In that case, a student (T.L.O.) was caught smoking at school in an undesignated zone. On the strength of that violation, a teacher searched her purse and found drug paraphernalia, marijuana, and evidence of drug sales. She was charged as a juvenile but fought the charges, arguing that the search of her purse violated her rights under the Fourth Amendment. The case made its way to the Supreme Court where in 1985 a 6–3 court ruled that while the prohibition against unreasonable searches does carry over to the schools, the search of T.L.O.'s purse was reasonable. The following comments by a law professor, excerpted from a publication for National School Resource Officers, provides guidance to schools on privacy rights in school. Throughout the article, you will see references to the TLO case.*

Reform in education law continues to give school officials broad authority to implement policies that are designed to keep campuses safe. The primary reason for this trend is that each state, "having compelled students to attend school and thus associate with the criminal few—or perhaps merely the immature and unwise few—closely and daily, thereby owes those students a safe and secure environment."[1] The U.S. Supreme Court has held that, "maintaining security and order in the schools requires a certain degree of flexibility in school disciplinary procedures, and we have respected the value of preserving the informality of the student-teacher relationship" *[New Jersey v. TLO]*. Educators who take up this challenge find themselves under constant pressure to keep

---

[1] This quote is from W. LaFave, *Search & Seizure: A Treatise on the Fourth Amendment* (3rd ed. 1996), pp. 802-03.

their campus policies up-to-date in response to the evolving ways in which student conduct may conflict with a safe and effective learning environment.

New technology, including cell phones, pagers, and other personal digital assistants (PDAs) raise important questions about the authority of educators to seize, search, and inspect the contents of these devices when their possession or use violates school rules.

Do students have an expectation of privacy in these devices that outweighs the authority of educators to ban their possession and use on campus? If school codes may prohibit these devices, then may educators search the contents of seized devices? Does the law require educators to obtain a search warrant before the contents of the devices can be inspected? Or, may school officials rely on mere reasonable suspicion to inspect student devices that violate the code of conduct?

This topic is now a timely one. Many educators have prohibited possession and use of the devices on campus to eliminate disruptions, crimes, and harassment as well as to discourage cheating on exams. These educators routinely examine the confiscated phones. Other educators wish to do so, but are unclear as to what the law permits.

Lawyers for both schools and students frequently discuss the issue and disagree over what the law requires in this regard.

Test your "cell phone IQ" on the following scenarios.

1. A student is stopped in the hallway for being out of class between periods without the hall pass required by the code of conduct. The assistant principal searches the student and feels an object under the student's coat. The principal reaches into the coat and pulls out a cell phone in a case. The principal felt there was something in the case in addition to the phone, opened the case and found what was later determined to be heroin. The student was suspended and the police were called. Was the search of the cell phone case lawful?

2. A student was caught smoking in the bathroom in violation of school policy. The student's purse was searched by the principal who suspected her of having more cigarettes therein. The principal discovered cigarettes in her possession, and discovered the drug marijuana, a cell phone, and a written list of alleged users from the school. The principal believed that the cell phone contained information about drugs on campus and read several

text messages. The messages led the principal to other students who had drugs and a non-student who was the supplier of the drugs. The students were suspended and the police called to arrest the students. Is the search of the cell phone valid under the Fourth Amendment?

3. A student is taken to the principal's office after his pager starts ringing in class. Possession of pagers and cell phones is prohibited by the school code of conduct. The principal seized and made a list of the telephone numbers stored in the student's pager. Is this search valid without a search warrant?

4. While patrolling campus during the school day, an SRO [School Resource Officer] observes a student talking on a cell phone in the campus parking lot. Possession and use of a cell phone during the school day is a violation of the school code of conduct. The student was brought to the office of the principal, who examined the cell phone. He observed numerous calls logged on the caller ID screen. While reviewing the contents of the phone, it began ringing. When the phone rang, the principal flipped it open, activating the backlight. He observed a "wallpaper" photo of another student who was the caller. It was later determined that the caller was truant from school. Is this handling of the phone valid?

In a 1983 case, *United States v. Place*, the Supreme Court ruled that the sniff of a police dog authorized to be in a common area is not a search in the Fourth Amendment sense of the word and therefore does not require a warrant.

The Standards for Searching Student Property

Under the Fourth Amendment, searches and seizures must be "reasonable." There are at least two branches of reasonableness jurisprudence.[2] Under the criminal law branch a reasonable search must be based on probable cause to believe that a violation of the law has occurred and a search warrant. However, under the education law branch neither probable cause nor a warrant is required. The U.S. Supreme Court has decided that, "[t]he accommodation of . . . the substantial need of teachers and administrators for freedom to maintain order in the schools does not require strict adherence to the requirement that searches be based on probable cause" [TLO]. Instead, the following rules govern.

> Determining the reasonableness of [a student] search involves a twofold inquiry: first, one must consider "whether the . . . action was justified at its inception"; [and] second, one must determine whether the search as actually conducted "was reasonably related in scope to the circumstances which justified the interference in the first place." Under ordinary circumstances, a search of a student by a teacher or other school official will be "justified at its inception" when there are reasonable grounds for suspecting that the search will turn up evidence that the student has violated or is violating either the law or the rules of the school. Such a search will be permissible in its scope when the measures adopted are reasonably related to the objectives of the search and not excessively intrusive in light of the age and sex of the student and the nature of the infraction [TLO].

Under these guidelines, those arguing against the validity of content searches of confiscated phones assume a heavy burden of persuasion because current judicial attitudes uphold school policies that are designed to uncover and prevent misconduct by students that, "materially disrup[t] classwork or involv[e] substantial disorder or invasion of the rights of others" [Tinker v. Des Moines, 1969]. The TLO standard has been applied to uphold a broad range of content searches that are difficult to distinguish from the search of a phone. The contents of lockers, purses, backpacks, cars, and clothing have all been upheld when the educator

---

2 **reasonableness jurisprudence:** the category of laws and cases that deals with determining reasonableness

has a reasonable suspicion for suspecting that the student has violated or is violating either the law or the rules of the school.

When applied to cell phone searches, it is clear that the initial seizure and search that occurs when a student is found in possession (and or use) of a phone in violation of school policy is justified at its inception. Students have no immunity from the seizure or the search of a phone or PDA which school officials have prohibited from campus. Possession of the phone in violation of school rules supports, at a minimum, an inquiry (as to both the student and the phone) to determine the circumstances of its possession and the uses, if any, to which it has been put that affect the campus. Indeed, when *TLO* is faithfully applied to school policies of cell phones and other devices, then the focus will be not on whether such a search is justified at its inception, but on the scope of the search. How far can an educator go in harvesting the contents of a phone before it is no longer (to use the words of *TLO),* "reasonably related in scope to the circumstances which justified the interference in the first place?"

At one end of the "how far can the educator go" issue, some content searches of a phone will not be controversial at all. For example, an educator who examines the contents of a phone in order to determine its true owner would be acting under the best of our traditions in public education. So, too, a teacher who handles and examines a phone that is receiving a call, delivering a message, or signaling an alarm, would not be second-guessed. The searches in these examples are directly related in scope to the interest of the educator to make an accurate assessment of the nature of the disruption and its risk to the school. Beyond these "safe" scenarios lies considerable discomfort and disagreement over both the legality and the wisdom of content searches of phones that harvest the contents of a confiscated phone. . . .

The answers to the questions in the I.Q. test are all "yes." . . .

Adult Time for Adult Crimes

Charles D. Stimson and Andrew M. Grossman

The final set of readings examines the issue of punishment for juvenile offenders. The first is from a 2009 report by the Heritage Foundation, a conservative "think tank" that promotes traditional values. It refers to a 2005 Supreme Court decision in Roper v. Simmons, *in which the Court held that the death penalty for people who committed crimes when they were juveniles violated their Eighth Amendment right to protection from "cruel and unusual punishment." The report argues that efforts to extend that ruling to a lesser sentence of life without parole are misguided.*

A Small but Coordinated Movement

Opponents of tough sentences for serious juvenile offenders have been working for years to abolish the sentence of life without the possibility of parole. Though representing relatively few, these groups are highly organized, well-funded, and passionate about their cause. Emboldened by the Supreme Court's decision in *Roper,* which relied on the "cruel and unusual punishments" language of the Eighth Amendment to the Constitution to prohibit capital sentences for juveniles, they have set about to extend the result of *Roper* to life without parole.

These groups wrap their reports and other products in the language of *Roper* and employ sympathetic terms like "child" and "children" and Roper-like language such as "death sentence" instead of the actual sentence of life without parole. Their reports are adorned with pictures of children, most of whom appear to be five to eight years old, despite the fact that the youngest person serving life without parole in the United States is 14 years old and most are 17 or 18 years old.

A careful reading of these groups' reports, articles, and press releases reveals that their messages and themes have been tightly coordinated. There is a very unsubtle similarity in terminology among organizations in characterizing the sentence of life without parole for juvenile offenders. For example, they consistently decline to label teenage offenders "juveniles" despite the fact that the term is used by the states, lawyers, prosecutors, state statutes, judges, parole officers, and everyone else in the juvenile justice system. Instead, they use "child."

There is nothing wrong, of course, with advocacy groups coordinating their language and message. The problem is that this important public policy debate has been shaped by a carefully crafted campaign of misinformation.

The issue of juvenile offenders and the proper sentence they are due is much too important to be driven by manufactured statistics, a misreading of a Supreme Court case, and fallacious[1] assertions that the United States is in violation of international law. Instead, the debate should be based on real facts and statistics, a proper reading of precedent, an intelligent understanding of federal and state sovereignty, and a proper understanding of our actual international obligations.

The Public Is Disserved by a One-Sided Debate

Regrettably, that has not been the case, as opponents of life without parole for juvenile offenders have monopolized the debate. As a result, legislatures, courts, the media, and the public have been misled on crucial points.

One prominent example is a frequently cited statistic on the number of juvenile offenders currently serving life-without-parole sentences. Nearly all reports published on the subject and dozens of newscasts and articles based on those reports state that there are at least 2,225 juveniles sentenced to life without parole. That number first appeared in a 2005 report by Amnesty International and Human Rights Watch, *The Rest of Their Lives: Life Without Parole for Child Offenders in the United States*.

---

1   **fallacious:** arrived at through faulty logic

But a careful look at the data and consultation with primary sources—that is, state criminal-justice officials—reveals that this statistic is seriously flawed. As described below, officials in some states reject as incorrect the figures assigned to their states. Others admit that they have no way of knowing how many juvenile offenders in their states have been sentenced to life without parole—and that, by extension, neither could activist groups.

Nonetheless, this statistic has gone unchallenged even as it has been cited in appellate briefs[2] and oral arguments before state supreme courts and even in a petition to the United States Supreme Court. All of these courts have been asked to make public policy based on factual representations that even cursory[3] research would demonstrate are questionable.

Another example is the unrealistic portrait of the juvenile offenders who are sentenced to life without parole that activist groups have painted. Nearly every report contains sympathetic summaries of juvenile offenders' cases that gloss over the real facts of the crimes, deploying lawyerly language and euphemism[4] to disguise brutality and violence.

In a similar vein, many of the studies feature pictures of children who are far younger than any person actually serving life without parole in the United States. When these reports do include an actual picture of a juvenile offender, the picture is often one taken years before the crime was committed. The public could be forgiven for believing incorrectly that children under 14 are regularly sentenced to life behind bars without the possibility of release. . . .

A final example is the legality of life-without-parole sentences for juvenile offenders. Opponents make the claim, among many others, that these sentences violate the United States' obligations under international law. Yet they usually fail to mention that no court has endorsed this view, and rarely do they explain the implications of the fact that the United States has not ratified the treaty that they most often cite, the Convention on the Rights of the Child, and has carved out legal exceptions (called "reservations") to others.

Further, they often abuse judicial precedent by improperly extending the death penalty-specific logic and language of *Roper* into the non-death

---

2 **appellate briefs:** written arguments requesting an appeal
3 **cursory:** hasty and shallow
4 **euphemism:** language designed to represent something unpleasant in softer terms

penalty arena, an approach that the Supreme Court has repeatedly rejected. Again, the public could be forgiven for believing incorrectly that the Supreme Court, particularly in *Roper,* has all but declared the imposition of life sentences without parole for juvenile offenders to be unconstitutional. A more honest reading of the precedent, however, compels the opposite conclusion: that the sentence is not constitutionally suspect.

The Whole Story

Public policy should be based on facts, not false statistics and misleading legal claims. For that reason, we undertook the research to identify those states that have authorized life without parole for juvenile offenders and wrote to every major district attorney's office across those 43 states. To understand how prosecutors are using life-without-parole sentences and the types of crimes and criminals for which such sentences are imposed, we asked each office for case digests of juvenile offenders who were prosecuted by their offices and received the specific sentence of life without parole.

The response from prosecutors around the country was overwhelming. Prosecutors from across the United States sent us case digests, including official court documents, police reports, judges' findings, photos of the defendants and victims, motions, newspaper articles, and more. From that collection of case digests, we selected 16 typical cases, all concerning juvenile offenders, and assembled a complete record for each. Those cases are presented as studies [elsewhere] in this report. In sharp contrast to the practices of other reports, these case studies recount all of the relevant facts of the crimes, as found by a jury or judge and recorded in official records (which are cited), in neutral language.

The text of the report itself includes a neutral analysis of the relevant case law and Supreme Court precedents, as well as an analysis of how international law affects domestic practice in this area. It also includes a rough analysis (which is all the present data will allow) of the statistics often used in activist groups' reports and a comparison of U.S. and international juvenile crime statistics.

Based on this research, we conclude that the sentence of life without parole for juvenile offenders is reasonable, constitutional, and (appropriately) rare. Our survey of the cases shows that some juveniles commit horrific crimes with full knowledge of their actions and intent to bring about the results. In constitutional terms, the Supreme Court's own jurisprudence, including *Roper,* draws a clear line between the sentence of death and all others, including life without parole; further, to reach its result, *Roper* actually depends on the availability of life without parole for juvenile offenders. We also find that while most states allow life-without-parole sentences for juvenile offenders, judges generally have broad discretion in sentencing, and most juvenile offenders do not receive that sentence.

We conclude, then, that reports by activist groups on life without parole for juvenile offenders are at best misleading and in some instances simply wrong in their facts, analyses, conclusions, and recommendations. Regrettably, the claims made by these groups have been repeated so frequently that lawmakers, judges, the media, and the public risk losing sight of their significant bias.

To foster informed debate, more facts—particularly, good state-level statistics—are needed about the use of life-without-parole sentences for juvenile offenders. But even on the basis of current data, as insufficient as they are, legislators should take note of how these sentences are actually applied and reject any attempts to repeal life-without-parole sentences for juvenile offenders.

JUVENILE JUSTICE

In January 2001, the investigative documentary series Frontline *on Public Broadcasting Service aired a show examining the difficult question of how juveniles who commit serious crimes should be treated in the legal system. How are the views here similar to and different from the views in the report by the Heritage Foundation?*

Should teenagers who commit violent or serious crimes be tried as juveniles or adults? Can we rehabilitate these young people to prevent future criminal behavior? With almost unprecedented access to juvenile court proceedings—which are usually closed to the public and rarely seen on television—"Juvenile Justice" follows four youth offenders through the Santa Clara County, California, juvenile courts, observing how the criminal justice system treats their cases and determines their fates. Filmed over 15 months, this report also talks with the judges, case workers, prosecutors, and families of the young teens as well as some of those who were their victims.

We meet Manny, 17, charged with the attempted murder of a pregnant woman and her family; José, a 15-year-old gang member sentenced to Juvenile Hall for his role in the beating death of another teen; Shawn, a middle-class white teen who pleaded guilty to trying to murder his father; and Marquese, an African-American teen who has seven felonies on his record, all theft related.

"While their crimes are different and they come from diverse backgrounds, these four teens are all united by the fact that they each are at a crossroads in the system," says FRONTLINE producer Janet Tobias. "One road leads to rehabilitation in the juvenile system; the other leads to punishment in the adult system."[1]

In the past decade, nearly every state in the union has passed laws or amended legislation to make it easier to prosecute and sentence children as adults. Proponents of these tougher policies say they're fed up with a system that offers little more than a slap on the wrist to children who commit serious crimes. Some even question whether repeated attempts to rehabilitate habitual youth offenders are serving the interests of overall justice.

But others aren't so sure. FRONTLINE interviews juvenile court judges and attorneys, who, although disagreeing on some points, do agree that decisions about which kids to treat as kids and which should be sent to adult court are very difficult.

Former public defender Bridgett Jones is one who believes the system needs to distinguish between juvenile and adult offenders. "Children are not little adults," she says. "They think differently. They respond and react to things differently than adults do. . . .So why should the consequences be the same as for an adult?"

---

1 Manny and José ended up in adult court. **Manny** was sentenced to 9 years in prison in 2001. With two adult violent convictions already by the age of 18, he doubted he would avoid life imprisonment because of California's "three-strike" rule. **José** now has an adult record as well, though he served his time in juvenile hall where he appeared to turn himself around. However, he was arrested after his release from juvenile hall in January 2001 for violation of his probation. Shawn and Marquese ended up in juvenile court. **Shawn** had to stay in juvenile hall until age 19, but during his time there he was able to leave during the day for classes at community college, counseling, and even meals with his family. Many people thought because of his race and economic status he had been given special treatment. He was back in trouble for probation violation months after his release. The judge in **Marquese's** case decided to return 17-year-old Marquese to the juvenile system for one last chance at rehabilitation, based on the horrendous circumstances of his upbringing, with a mother addicted to heroin and crack cocaine and in and out of jail herself. Marquese's crimes were also nonviolent.

California prosecutor David Soares disagrees. "The voters in this state and the legislature have decided that . . . there are many 15-year-olds and 16-year-olds and 17-year-olds and 18-year-olds who are as intellectually and criminally sophisticated as adult offenders," he says. "And the decisions that have been made by our lawmakers and by the voters are that we look at their actions and [determine] are they engaging in the actions of an adult."

At issue is whether the juvenile justice system has been—or even can be—successful in rehabilitating young criminals. And if they can be rehabilitated, will it be enough to regain society's trust? It's a question even some youth offenders have trouble answering. "Even if I want to change, people are still gonna look at me like I'm a gangster," says Manny, the teen charged with attempted murder.

Therein lies the problem, public defender Jones says. "The only thing that's going to work with kids like [these] is a willingness of the community to redeem them and saying, 'Look, your life's not over, there's still hope for you.'"

Interviews with Judges and Attorneys

Judge Thomas Edwards Until recently he was the presiding judge of the Juvenile Court of Santa Clara County, a division of the California Superior Court, and presided over Shawn's case. He heard between 300 and 350 cases a month.

Are there kids that don't belong in juvenile court?

Oh, sure. Yes. I've had sociopaths[2] in court here. I've had only a few of them, and I've been doing this for a long time. I can only really count maybe a half a dozen, and only two in particular that I would be very frightened to see on the street. But I see them from time to time.

Some people believe that no kid belongs in adult court. For one reason, they can't be tried by a jury of their peers, because people of their age are not allowed to serve. And some people would argue that, just by definition, they cannot receive a fair hearing in adult court because of that. What do you think?

---

2 **sociopaths:** people with a personality disorder capable of extreme behavior and lacking a conscience for any wrongdoing

They may be right.

Knowing what you know about the lack of services if a child is convicted in adult court, knowing that there aren't going to be the kinds of counseling and therapeutic and educational services available, do you feel, in essence, that you're writing somebody off when you send them off?

Oh, absolutely. Yes. It's not a good feeling. It hurts.

When you have a kid who has committed a serious offense, someone who's caused harm—most likely a crime of violence— what makes you keep them in the juvenile system?

I'll keep them if I think I can make a difference. And the difference may not manifest itself for many, many years. But if I think there is a good likelihood that we can get this kid off the path he's on and onto a better path, then it's worth the time and the effort. Even if it's a long shot, I'm willing to take it.

Bridgett Jones Former supervisor of the juvenile division of the Santa Clara County Public Defender's Office, she represented Shawn at his disposition.

Does any kid belong in the adult criminal system?

That's a hard question, and the reason it's a hard question is because systemically,[3] my belief is we could do it all better. . . . I don't think a lot of adults belong in adult detention, quite frankly. I think we could do a better job with that. If you look at recidivism[4] rates throughout the country, this punitive system is not working. It doesn't work. From one standpoint, if you lock people up for life and they never get out, I guess you could say that works in terms of public safety as to that person, but it certainly has not proven to have any impact on recidivism. . . . So we have this incredibly ineffective adult system, and now we

---

3 **systemically:** throughout the system
4 **recidivism:** return to criminal behavior

want to take kids, and put them into what we already know is ineffective. . . . Why? Why? That makes no sense to me. We want to replicate what we're doing for adults, which we know doesn't work, for kids, when we have an opportunity to possibly impact their lives.

Now, another way of getting at that same question is that I do feel that there are people that are so damaged that they are damaged beyond repair, that there's not a good intervention that you can do to salvage them. Whatever their internal stuff is that enables them to connect in a meaningful way, it's broken. But I think that's a very small, I mean extremely small, percentage of people that I've run across, especially in the juvenile system.

Judge LaDoris Cordell Until recently she served on the Superior Court of Santa Clara County, where she heard both juvenile and adult cases. A state court trial judge since 1982, she presided over Manny's fitness case.[5]

Do you think any kid ever belongs in adult court?

Yes. . . . I have come across some young people who are so sophisticated and who have committed such heinous[6] crimes that the adult system is the place for them to be. I haven't come across a lot, but there have been some. . . . It can happen, and it does happen. . . .

Kurt Kumli The supervising deputy district attorney for the Juvenile Division of the Santa Clara County's District Attorney's office, he's practiced exclusively in juvenile court for the past six years. He was the prosecutor for Manny's fitness hearing.

If we could take every kid and surround the kid with full-time staffs of psychologists and child advocates and drug and alcohol counselors, then perhaps no kid should be in adult court. But the fact is, there are only a limited number

---

5 **fitness case:** a case to determine whether the accused was fit to be tried as a juvenile
6 **heinous:** hideous; abhorrent

of resources in the juvenile justice system, and they can only perform a limited number of functions. To optimize those services for the kids that can benefit the greatest amount from them, you have to make the hard call, sometimes, as to whether or not the high-end offenders—and again, we are only talking about the one or two percent of kids who ever come into the system—whether those kids really are the just recipients of the resources that the juvenile justice system has available to it. . . .

Responding to Cluster Four

Thinking on Your Own

Critical Thinking Skill INTEGRATING SOURCES OF INFORMATION

1. Several phrases taken from the landmark case *Tinker v. Des Moines* have created a judicial precedent for future cases. For example, students do not "shed their constitutional rights to freedom of speech or expression at the schoolhouse gate." Student expression may not be suppressed unless it will "materially and substantially disrupt the work and discipline of the school." "First amendment rights, applied in light of the special characteristics of the school environment, are available to teachers and students." How has the meaning of specific parts of these statements been clarified and applied to subsequent court cases? Integrate information from the selections found in this cluster as you fill in the following chart.

Language/concept from *Tinker v. Des Moines*	Description of case	Clarification and application
"schoolhouse gate"		
"materially and substantially disrupt"		
"special characteristics of the school environment"		

2. Explain in detail the argument Justice Roberts makes in "Student Speech Can Be Restricted." Evaluate how he applies the Constitution and uses legal reasoning.

3. Why are the school's actions in "Webcamgate" considered an invasion of privacy, but the searching of cell phones in *New Jersey v. TLO* (and in the four examples on pages 125–126) are not? Explain the arguments used by the courts by citing specific details.

4. What are the fundamental issues in the debate of how to deal with juvenile offenders? Integrate information from "Adult Time for Adult Crimes" and "Juvenile Justice" in your answer.

Writing Activity: Integrate Sources in an Argument

With a partner, choose one of the Supreme Court cases mentioned in this cluster or another landmark case dealing with individual rights. Conduct research on the case, including reading majority and dissenting opinions. Have each partner take a position on the case and write a two- to three-page argument that integrates his or her research. Read the essays aloud to the class and discuss the strengths and weaknesses of the arguments.

A Strong Argument

- introduces clear claims
- supports claims with logical reasons, accurate data, and relevant evidence from credible sources
- acknowledges and addresses counterclaims

AUTHOR BIOGRAPHIES

Akhil Reed Amar Akhil Reed Amar is a professor of law and political science at Yale University. He served as a clerk to Judge Stephen Breyer, U.S. Court of Appeals, 1st Circuit, and has written or edited many highly regarded books on the Constitution, including *America's Constitution: A Biography* (Random House, 2005). The Supreme Court has referred to his work in more than 20 cases. Amar also worked as a consultant to the television show *The West Wing* to help make presentation of Constitutional issues as accurate as possible.

Linda Chavez Linda Chavez is a political columnist, radio commentator, and analyst on Fox Television. Under Presidents Ronald Reagan and George W. Bush, she served in key positions related to civil rights and immigration. In 2000, she was named one of the Library of Congress Living Legends.

James A. Emanuel James A. Emanuel has been called one of the best and most neglected living poets. He has published more than 300 poems and has also written a biography of Langston Hughes, whom he regarded as his mentor.

Abdus Sattar Ghazali Abdus Sattar Ghazali is an author and journalist specializing in Islam in today's world. He is the author of *Islamic Pakistan: Illusions & Reality; Islam in the Post-Cold War Era; Islam & Modernism;* and *Islam & Muslims in Post-9/11 America.* He served from 1969 to 1976 as a news editor for the Daily News, Kuwait. He joined the English News Department of Kuwait Television as a news editor in December 1976. He retired in 1998 as the editor-in-chief of the Kuwait Television English News. Ghazali also worked as a correspondent of the Associated Press of Pakistan in Kuwait. He is currently the executive editor of the online journal *American Muslim Perspective.*

Arthur Goldberg Arthur Goldberg (1908–1990), the son of a fruit peddler, had a keen awareness of privileges denied to the poor. When just 15, he became fascinated with the trial of Leopold and Loeb, wealthy young men who were spared the death penalty for the murder of a 14-year-old boy. His interest in that case was part of his inspiration for pursuing a career in law. Later, when he was on the Supreme Court (1965–1968), he expressed the view that because capital punishment is applied more often to the poor or to those of a lower social status, the Court should consider the constitutionality of the death penalty. Goldberg is also known for his support of organized labor. He worked for several large labor unions and also served as Secretary of Labor under President Kennedy.

Andrew M. Grossman Andrew Grossman is an award-winning visiting fellow at The Heritage Foundation's Center for Legal and Judicial Studies. He also practices law with a Washington, D.C., firm and has expert experience handling cases that focus on the Constitution's limits on federal power. He has advised Congress on a number of cases and written numerous briefs for the Supreme Court. His commentaries appear regularly in leading newspapers, and he is a regular legal commentator on a number of television and radio stations.

Learned Hand Billings Learned Hand (1872–1961) was a federal judge who became widely known outside of the legal realm after his famous "Spirit of Liberty" speech in New York City. He became known as a staunch defender of free speech and other civil liberties, and his opinions and other legal writings set a standard for legal craft and eloquence.

Beth Hawkins Beth Hawkins is an award-winning journalist from Minneapolis, Minnesota. Now a freelance journalist covering education and public policy for minnpost.com, an online daily, Hawkins has worked previously as senior editor at the Minneapolis *City Pages* and managing editor at Detroit's *Metro Times*. She also covers court cases for Bloomberg News, a news outlet specializing in financial news.

Nat Hentoff Nat Hentoff is a prolific writer noted for his novels, biographies, books on jazz, and writings on First Amendment rights. He was a staff writer for the *New Yorker* for 25 years and contributed a widely distributed weekly column called "Sweet Land of Liberty" to the *Village Voice* newspaper from 1957–2008. He has been a Senior Fellow at the Cato Institute since 2009.

Laura Hershey Laura Hershey (1962–2010) was a poet, writer, speaker, and activist who worked for rights for people with disabilities. Hershey had muscular dystrophy and as a child represented the face of muscular dystrophy for the Jerry Lewis telethon. She later protested against the telethons of the Muscular Dystrophy Association, arguing that they portrayed people with disabilities as weak and unable to live full lives without a "cure." Hershey contributed a regular column to *Crip Commentary,* the publication of the Christopher and Dana Reeve Foundation. She also wrote numerous articles for a variety of publications and was in demand as a speaker.

Bernard James Bernard James is professor of Law at Pepperdine University School of Law. He is an expert in education and the law and also serves as consultant to the U.S. Department of Justice where he has specialized in juvenile justice. At Pepperdine he concentrates on constitutional matters and has a special expertise in the First Amendment. He has provided media commentary both locally and nationally on constitutional law.

Thomas Jefferson Third president of the United States, Thomas Jefferson (1743–1826) has had enormous and enduring influence on the character of the nation. Religious freedom was an essential democratic principle to Jefferson. When he designed his tombstone and wrote his epitaph as his death approached, he included only three accomplishments on it: "Author of the Declaration of Independence, [and] of the Statute of Virginia for religious freedom & Father of the University of Virginia." Jefferson scholar Merrill D. Peterson called the Virginia statute "one of the main pillars of American democracy and a beacon of light and liberty to the world."

Anthony Lewis A two-time Pulitzer-prize winner, Anthony Lewis has a long history in journalism and letters, having worked for the *New York Times* in a variety of capacities, taught at Columbia University's Graduate School of Journalism, and written such books as *Gideon's Trumpet* and *Freedom for the Thought That We Hate,* from which the selection in this book is taken. During the McCarthy era, Lewis's reporting salvaged the job of a U.S. Navy employee who had been fired on suspicion of being a communist sympathizer. He also covered the Supreme Court. In 2001, President Clinton awarded him the Presidential Citizens Medal for being "a clear and courageous voice for democracy and justice."

Heather Mac Donald Heather Mac Donald is a fellow at the Manhattan Institute for Policy Research and contributes to its publication *City Journal,* which is devoted to exploring the challenges of modern urban life and examining possible solutions. Mac Donald is an award-winning columnist and writer who has testified before Congress on homeland security and immigration issues. In contrast to many other conservative commentators, Mac Donald is an atheist and feels that conservative ideas are sufficiently strong to prove superior to liberal ideas on their own merits and that religion should not play a part in them.

James Madison By the time he was 25, James Madison (1751–1836) had already become a leader in Virginia politics and was starting his distinguished career. Over the next four decades, he served in the Virginia state legislature, in the U.S. House of Representatives, as secretary of state, and as President. But his most notable contribution came in 1787 and 1788. No other delegate to the Constitutional Convention did as much as he did to shape the compromises in the Constitution, and no one did as much as he did later to advocate for its ratification. An ardent Republican, he matched his fear of tyranny with a recognition of the value of a strong federal government.

Alexis Madrigal Alexis Madrigal is a senior editor at *The Atlantic* and a visiting professor at the University of California-Berkeley. He also worked as a staff writer at Wired.com, where he made frequent contributions to Wired Science. At *The Atlantic,* he created the magazine's online Technology Channel, where he and others explore the impact of technology on humans and their environments. Madrigal's book, *Powering the Dream: The History and Promise of Green Technology*, was published in 2010.

Newton R. Minow While chairman of the Federal Communications Commission (1961–1963), Newton Minow issued a challenge to the leaders of the television industry: "sit down in front of your television set when your station goes on the air and stay there without a book, magazine, newspaper, profit-and-loss sheet or rating book to distract you—and keep your eyes glued to that set until the station signs off. I can assure you that you will observe a vast wasteland." Among other concerns, Minow feared that television had become a form of escapism that was keeping people from getting involved in public life in meaningful ways. In his long and distinguished career, Minow has had executive positions with Encyclopedia Britannica and the law firm of Sidley and Austin and has been a professor of communications policy and law at Northwestern University. He has served on the boards of Public Broadcasting Services, Jewish Theological Seminary, and a number of other institutions of higher learning.

Linda R. Monk Linda R. Monk, J.D., is an award-winning constitutional scholar, journalist, and author. A graduate of Harvard Law School, Monk reaches out to readers with history and explanations of the various clauses in the Constitution and amendments. Her books include *The Words We Live By: Your Annotated Guide to the Constitution; Ordinary Americans: U.S. History Through the Eyes of Everyday People;* and *The Bill of Rights: A User's Guide,* from which the selection in this book is taken. Monk also writes commentary for national newspapers, including the *New York Times, Washington Post,* and *Chicago Tribune.*

Aquiles Nazoa Aquiles Nazoa (1920–1976) was a beloved Venezuelan poet and humorist known for his gentle love of children and animals and the beauty of simple everyday things. At the same time, he was outspoken about freedoms, and in his role as correspondent for *El Universal,* a Caracas newspaper, he criticized authorities in the northern city of Puerto Cabello when he felt their actions were wrong—and he paid the price by being arrested in 1940 for slander and defamation. He was expelled from Venezuela in 1956 by the military regime in power but returned in 1958. He died in a car crash in 1976.

George Orwell Eric Arthur Blair (1903–1950), pen name George Orwell, wrote novels (*Animal Farm* and *Nineteen Eighty-Four* among them), literary criticism, and essays. In his essay "Politics and the English Language" (1946), he criticizes political writing for its effort "to make lies sound truthful and murder respectable. . . ." Orwell was a strong critic of such totalitarian regimes as Stalin's Soviet Union, on which he based several aspects of the gray society of *Nineteen Eighty-Four.* So effective was his ability to paint the dystopian society of *Nineteen Eighty-Four* that governments or governmental actions that resemble that society are now described as Orwellian.

John Roberts President George W. Bush appointed John Roberts Chief Justice of the Supreme Court in 2005. Like a number of his colleagues on the Supreme Court, Roberts graduated from Harvard Law School. He worked in several different capacities in the Reagan and Bush administrations, and then, in private practice, argued a number of cases in the Supreme Court, winning many of them. During his confirmation hearings as a nominee for the Supreme Court, Roberts stressed that individual beliefs are not a highly relevant concern: "[J]udges wear black robes because it doesn't matter who they are as individuals. That's not going to shape their decision. It's their understanding of the law that will shape their decision."

Mario Rodriguez Mario Rodriguez is a doctoral candidate at the University of Pennsylvania's Annenberg School for Communication specializing in social network privacy. To obtain his Ph.D., he is studying the Facebook behavior of college seniors as they enter the job market to see if and how they may change their levels of privacy. Rodriguez was a Media Fellow in the office of Bernard Sanders, the U.S. senator from Vermont, and has also worked as a journalist.

Margaret Chase Smith In 1940, when her husband U.S. Representative Clyde Smith of Maine became too ill to serve, Margaret Chase Smith (1897–1995) was elected to finish out his term. After he died, she was elected time and again to public office on her own merits, becoming the first woman to serve in both the House of Representatives and the Senate. It was on the Senate floor that Chase made her famous "Declaration of Conscience" speech in 1950. She ran an unsuccessful campaign for the presidency in 1964, not the first time she helped blaze a trail for women in traditionally male positions.

Sonia Sotomayor Associate Supreme Court Justice Sonia Sotomayor, the first Hispanic to sit on the Court, traveled a long way from her upbringing in a South Bronx housing project to her appointment to the Supreme Court in 2009. She graduated with high honors from Princeton as an undergraduate and received her degree in law from Yale Law School. She began her work as a prosecutor in criminal cases in Manhattan, focusing on such street crimes as murders, robberies, child abuse, police misconduct, and fraud. After working in private law for eight years, she got the first of her presidential appointments to serve as a federal judge. During her confirmation hearings for Supreme Court Justice, Senator Patrick Leahy (D., Vt.) said that Sotomayor "understands there's not one law for one race or another, there's not one law for one color or another, there's not one law for rich and a different one for poor. There's only one law."

Charles D. Stimson Charles Stimson is a Senior Legal Fellow at The Heritage Foundation's Center for Legal and Judicial Studies. He was formerly the Deputy Assistant Secretary of Defense for Detainee Affairs at the Pentagon and is a decorated military veteran. He is also an accomplished trial lawyer whose work as a criminal prosecutor concentrated on violent crimes, domestic violence cases, and homicides.

George Washington An inspiring military leader and the nation's first president, George Washington (1732–1799) set the precedent for future presidents with each step he took. While he wanted to establish a formal presidency to give the office dignity and authority, he preferred the now accepted form of address "Mr. President" to the more majestic titles suggested. He wanted to be clear in everything he did that the new nation was a republic, very different from the European monarchies of the time.

Dale Wisely Dale Wisely is a clinical psychologist and a K–12 school system director in Alabama.

ADDITIONAL READING

Battle for the Black Ballot, by Charles L. Zeldon. An account of the Supreme Court decision in *Smith v. Allwright* paving the way for African American voting rights in Texas—and throughout the nation. (2005)

The Battle Over School Prayer: How Engel v. Vitale *Changed America,* by Bruce J. Dierenfield. A guide to the case that became known as the "moment when the U.S. Supreme Court kicked God out of the public schools" in its ruling outlawing prayer in school. (2007)

The Bill of Rights: Creation and Reconstruction, by Akhil Reed Amar. A unique analysis of the Bill of Rights by a renowned Constitutional scholar, arguing that it wasn't until the introduction of the Fourteenth Amendment that the Bill of Rights took on the character of protecting individual rights as opposed to empowering popular majorities. (2000)

The Dark Side: The Inside Story of How the War on Terror Turned into a War on American Ideals, by Jane Mayer. A highly rated and carefully researched exposé of the excesses of the war on terror by a correspondent for *New Yorker* magazine. (2008)

In Defense of Liberty: The Story of America's Bill of Rights, by Russell Freedman. A look at the evolution of civil liberties through an amendment-by-amendment analysis, with both historical and modern examples and scenarios. (2003)

The Founders' Second Amendment: Origins of the Right to Bear Arms, by Stephen P. Halbrook. A close look at the world in which the framers lived in an effort to understand their intention with the Second Amendment. It does not include the latest rulings *(District of Columbia v. Heller* and *Chicago v. McDonald)* but nonetheless emphasizes the individual rights approach to understanding the Second Amendment. (2008)

Freedom: Stories Celebrating the Universal Declaration of Human Rights, Amnesty International USA. A collection of stories by leading authors from around the world highlighting the gains in individual rights internationally in the 60 years since the Universal Declaration of Human Rights was adopted by the United Nations.

Gideon's Trumpet, by Anthony Lewis. The classic account of how petty thief Clarence Earl Gideon protected his right to legal counsel and with the representation of Abe Fortas, who later became a Supreme Court judge himself, established the precedent that poor people are entitled to legal counsel even if they cannot afford it. (1989)

Money, Politics, and the Constitution: Beyond Citizens United, edited by Monica Youn. A collection of essays by outstanding legal scholars examining the controversial Supreme Court decision in *Citizens United v. Federal Election Commission* that held that corporations and unions had, like people, a right to free speech, and that free speech can be expressed as campaign contributions. (2011)

The Original Constitution: What It Really Said and Meant, by Robert G. Natelson. A look at the Constitution from the perspective of the founders, which the author argues is much different from the interpreted Constitution in operation today. (2010)

Rethinking Juvenile Justice, by Elizabeth S. Scott and Laurence Steinberg. A reasoned proposal by scholars in law and adolescent development for an approach to juvenile justice that recognizes adolescence as a stage of development but also holds young people accountable. (2010)

We the Students: Supreme Court Cases for and About Students, by Jamin B. Ruskin. A compilation of Supreme Court cases organized into topics of interest to students, such as discipline, discrimination, harassment, and property searches, including the texts of the opinions as well as key dissents. (2008)

The Words We Live By: Your Annotated Guide to the Constitution, by Linda R. Monk. Analyzes the Constitution one line at a time, with fascinating background information and anecdotes. (2003)

Note: The Supreme Court opinions, concurring statements, and oral transcripts included in this book—as well as many other Supreme Court documents—can all be found at http://www.supremecourt.gov/. In the excerpts in this book, citations to Supreme Court cases have been shortened to their name and year.

Acknowledgments

Text Credits

"Adult Time for Adult Crimes" by Charles D. Stimson and Andrew M. Grossman. Reprinted by permission of The Heritage Foundation, Center for Legal and Judicial Studies. Copyright © 2009.

"Atoms vs. Bits: Your Phone in the Eyes of the Law" by Alexis Madrigal Copyright © 2011. Used by permission of the author.

"Banning the Veil" by Linda Chavez. Copyright © 2010 by Linda Chavez. Reprinted by permission of Creators Syndicate.

"The Civil Rights of American Muslims After 9/11" by Abdus Sattar Ghazali. Copyright © 2008 Abdus Sattar Ghazali. Reprinted by permission of the author.

"The Courage of Their Convictions: Fannie Lou Hamer" by Linda R. Monk. Reprinted with permission from *The Bill of Rights: A User's Guide,* 4th ed., pp. 234–35, copyright © 2004 by Linda R. Monk.

"The Doll Test and the Fourteenth Amendment" by Nat Hentoff. Copyright © 1998 by Nat Hentoff. Reprinted by permission of HarperCollins Publishers.

"Emmett Till" by James A. Emanuel. James A. Emanuel, *Whole Grain: Collected Poems, 1958–1989,* Lotus Press, 1991.

Excerpts from *NINETEEN EIGHTY-FOUR* by George Orwell. © 1949 by Harcourt, Inc. and renewed 1977 by Sonia Brownell Orwell, reprinted by permission of the publishers.

"Impartial Jurors, Impartial Juries" by Newton Minow. Reprinted by permission of the author.

"In Defense of the Patriot Act" by Heather Mac Donald. Copyright © 2003 by Heather Mac Donald. Reprinted by permission of the author.

"Irregular Verbs" by Aquiles Nazoa. Reprinted by kind permission of New Internationalist. Copyright New Internationalist. www.newint.org

"Juvenile Justice" Synopsis from WGBH's FRONTLINE Juvenile Justice Web site (http://www.pbs.org/wgbh/pages/frontline/shows/juvenile/etc/synopsis.html) © 1995–2011 WGBH Educational Foundation.

Putting the Second Amendment Second
AKHIL REED AMAR
Copyright © 2008 by Akhil Reed Amar, first published by The Slate Group, a Division of Washington Post Company. All Rights Reserved c/o Writers Representatives LLC, New York, NY, 10011. Published by permission of Akhil Reed Amar.

"The Rights of Americans with Disabilities" by Atlanta Legal Aid Society. Reprinted by permission of Atlanta Legal Aid Society.

"Safe Schools, Cell Phones, and the Fourth Amendment" by Bernard James. Reprinted by permission of the author. Copyright © 2009.

"The Spirit of Liberty" by Judge Learned Hand. Courtesy of Historical & Special Collections, Harvard Law School Library.

"Thoughts That We Hate" by Anthony Lewis. Reprinted with permission from *Freedom for the Thought That We Hate* by Anthony Lewis. Available from Basic Books, a member of The Perseus Books Group. Copyright © 2010.

"Tinker Case Guides Court as Student's Parody of Principal Is Ruled Protected Speech" by Beth Hawkins. Copyright Minnpost.

"'Webcamgate' Shows Youth Are Not Apathetic About Privacy" by Mario Rodriguez. Reprinted by permission of the author. Copyright © 2010.

"The Work of Brothers" by Dale Wisely. Reprinted by permission of the author. Copyright © 2002.

"You Get Proud by Practicing" by Laura Hershey. Used by permission. Copyright © 1991 by Laura Hershey; cripcommentary.com.

Every reasonable effort has been made to properly acknowledge ownership of all material used. Any omissions or mistakes are not intentional and, if brought to the publisher's attention, will be corrected in future editions.

Photo and Art Credits

Cover: © Diana Ong / Purestock / SuperStock; Page 4: © Bettmann / CORBIS; Page 9: dreamstime.com; Page 10: dreamstime.com; Page 11: Can't Win This Game / Wikimedia Commons; Page 12: Western History / Genealogy Dept., Denver Public Library; Page 12: Library of Congress; Page 12: stus.com; Page 13: Library of Congress; Page 13: Brendan Hoffman/Stringer / Getty Images News / Getty Images; Page 13: photos.com; Page 13: iStockphoto.com; Page 15: © Flip Schulke/CORBIS; Page 16: © Hulton-Deutsch Collection/CORBIS; Page 17: Library of Congress; Page 19: Alexey Sergee / www.asergeev.eom / Wikimedia Commons; Page 22: photos.com; Page 25: McCARTHYISM CARTOON, 1950. 'McCarthy Was Here.' American cartoon by Daniel R. Fitzpatrick, 1950, on the scurrilous allegations by Senator Joseph R. McCarthy that Communists had infiltrated the U.S. State Department. The Granger Collection, NY; Page 27: © Images.com/Corbis; Page 31: Charles Knoblock / Associated Press; Page 35: © Bettmann/CORBIS; Page 37: Mary Evans Picture Library/ARTHUR RACKHAM; Page 43: © PoodlesRock/Corbis; Page 49: © ART on FILE/CORBIS; Page 51: iStockphoto.com; Page 53: Library of Congress; Page 58: © Bettmann/CORBIS; Page 60: Library of Congress; Page 62: Moore, Henry (1898-1986), Gianni Dagli Orti / The Art Archive at Art Resource, NY / Reproduced by permission of The Henry Moore Foundation; Page 68: www.atlantalegalaid.org; Page 70: © Mark Peterson / CORBIS; Page 71: Robin Nelson; Page 72: laurahershey.com / Robin Stephens; Page 76: Jake Fuller; Page 82: © Images.com / CORBIS; Page 90: 2001 The Record (Bergen Co. NJ) / Contributor / Getty Images News; Page 98: © 2011 Mike Keeft / www.politicalcartoons.com; Page 100: © Ed Kashi / CORBIS; Page 107: iStockphoto.com; Page 109: © Bettmann / CORBIS; Page 112: © Bettmann / CORBIS; Page 112: Ricky Sencion; Page 117: Evan Vucci / Associated Press; Page 120: iStockphoto.com; Page 123: Associated Press; Page 126: Time & Life Pictures / Getty Images; Page 130: iStockphoto.com; Page 134: iStockphoto.com; Page 139: iStockphoto.com